Aryon's Spanking Stories

Aryon's Spanking Stories

by

Aryon Weblog Authors

First published in 2011 as a Lulu Enterprises trade paperback.

Manufacturing by Lulu Enterprises, Inc.
http://www.lulu.com

For more information on the author, visit http://**aryondenik.blogspot.com**

To all kinky people

Aryon's Spanking Stories is a work of complete fiction.
No character in the book is meant to represent
any real person, living or dead.

Aryon's Spanking Stories contains sexual fantasies.
In real life, always practice safe sex.

Contents

Introduction

I started Aryon's blog about spanking in 2002. The blog is in Czech, and you can find it on *http://aryondenik.blogspot.com/*.

The Czech Republic is a place favorable to spanking. After all, it is one of a few countries with an official spanking holiday. Rooted in our pre-Christian, perhaps Celtic, history, it falls on Easter Monday. On this day, boys and men go and whip girls and women so they will be fresh, pretty, and healthy all year long. The women are whipped with birch twigs, juniper branches, or even big wooden spoons.

You might have read about the Czech Republic in Niki Flynn's *Dances with Werewolves*. Niki is a "spanking" model and made several spanking movies with a Czech producer from Lupus Pictures.

Aryon's blog about spanking has been the most popular erotic blog in our country for several years, which just proves how popular spanking is. At present, there are about 250 stories on the blog, with several well-liked authors contributing to the blog regularly.

By agreement with the authors, I chose twenty-two stories for this book. In my choice of stories, I focused on a tapestry of different views on spanking. In this first compilation, I included only stories in which women are submissive. Next year, I would like to continue with another collection of stories, where I will include stories with submissive men.

The authors are Katarina, Avellana, Vendula, Tomas, Fulgur, and Aryon.

Katarina wrote "The Princess and the Pea," "ICQ," "Bodyguard," "A Different View," "Another Story from the Wild West," "Bodyguard II," "Ill-Mannered Blanche," "Pirates," "What If I …," "Bodyguard III," and "Countess."

Avellana wrote "At a Spa," "An Advertisement," and "A Present."

Vendula wrote "An Examination Period" and "Sisters."

Tomas wrote "A Thrashing on a Whipping Post" and "A Wife and a Housemaid"

Fulgur wrote "A Punishment."

Aryon wrote "On a Business Trip with Lenka."

If you have any suggestions or remarks apropos the book as a whole or the authors of the stories, feel free to write to *aryon111@gmail.com*. I will forward e-mails directed to authors. You can also find me on Twitter: *http://twitter.com/aryonStories*.

Enjoy yourself while reading the stories.

Aryon

Acknowledgments

I would like to express my thanks to the authors—Katarina, Avellana, Vendula, Tomas, and Fulgur—for writing stories people liked so I had a reason to include them in the book.

Thanks belong also to the readers of *Aryon's Diary of Spanking*. They read the stories and some gave constructive comments.

Big thanks also belong to our translator Katka Tomigová, who had a difficult task translating the stories from Czech to English.

Chapter One

The Princess and the Pea

Dear big children, quickly brush your small teeth and off to bed with you, preferably in twos. The story about the magic old man and the princess and the pea begins.

Beyond many forests and meadows and beyond numerous bodies of water, there once existed a contented kingdom. A contented king ruled there contentedly, contented people worked contentedly in the fields and workrooms, contented women gave birth to contented children—except for one child. The king's daughter was beyond the contented average. Here she didn't like this, there she didn't like that; here she wanted more, and there she wanted less. Then one day, her daddy woke up discontented, which disquieted him. When the king was not content, his land and people were not content, and that, he thought from his high and contented position, could never be permitted.

He meditated and wracked his brain to no avail. Suddenly an idea penetrated his thoughts, and the king was content again. Quickly he dressed and set out. At dawn, he reached the clearing. A little cottage stood there. The king knocked diffidently, and a dulcet voice asked him to enter.

"Good morning, magic man," the king said as he squirmed uncomfortably in the door.

"Oh, good morning, Philip. I thought you didn't remember me anymore, but it is good that you came to visit me. I am glad to see you; it's been ages. You are all grown." The gray-haired man laughed jovially, and the king blushed at the memory how a long time ago he, too, came to satisfaction here.

"Magic man, I have a favor to ask of you. In our kingdom, there is one discontented girl. She is beautiful like a honey flower, but she is often shrouded in discontent. To make things worse, she is my daughter. Old man, please help me," The king forced himself to speak.

"My dear Philip, you are very smart. You achieved satisfaction; even your daughter will manage it for sure. Send her for a ride, but before she leaves, let the horse smell this flower so it may find the way here. I will begin my work when she arrives. Don't be afraid of anything; everything will come to a contented end. The world rotates and things happen. Now go, your land needs you."

Content, the king thanked the man and left.

"Daddy, it's hot. I don't want to go for a ride. I won't go.," Radomila stamped her feet.

"But, Radomila, because of you, I had to go without leading the country for a while. I want you to go riding. Be so kind and allow it to your aging father."

With a loud sigh, she swung on the horse and, without waiting for her father, sped off at a gallop into the shadow of the forest. The king scrambled onto his dapple-grey horse, and with a contented smile, he set out on their journey. They passed meadows, forests, creeks, and mosses. The king reveled in the smell of woods and the shade of its arms. At the right moment, he stopped his horse and sent a silent farewell toward his daughter as she rode off.

Radomila was angry. She yelled at the horse to stop, but he ran on and on as the magic smell of the flower commanded. His steps ended at the small clearing. Cursing, the princess dismounted. The horse looked in the window at the old man, gave a loud neigh in greeting, and contentedly set off at a trot. Radomila thought the horse turned and sneered at her, but, she thought to herself, that was probably because of the long journey.

"Old man, lend me a horse. I want to go home." She stormed into his little room. He stared at her in surprise.

Gee, he thought to himself, *Philip should have brought her a long time ago.*

He held out his hand to welcome her. "Good afternoon, Radomila. It's nice to meet you."

She snorted derisively. "Didn't you hear me? I want a horse. Tell me how can I get home to the castle. I'm a princess." She lifted her little chin proudly.

"That I couldn't help but notice, child. Well, I will show you the way home when I want to, which means when I consider you a reformed and contented girl. Until then, you are my respectable guest.

Join me at the table and have a lunch with me." He offered her a chair and a plate of cabbage soup.

"Phe!" She left resolutely. Despite wading through bushes and dunking her legs in creeks, her steps always ended by the cottage. As evening set in, wolves howled, owls told of their night adventures, and the moon sketched magic pictures. Radomila was scared. She ran as fast as she could, fought thorn bushes, forced her way through branches, until finally, she ended up at the clearing again. When she entered the small room, the old man was sitting by the fire, classifying herbs.

"So, Radomila, did you have a nice walk?"

"I would like a horse. On foot, the journey doesn't go very well. Give me a horse." She held a painted pitcher in her hand, and with a nice backswing, she threw it on the floor. The magic old man, however, waved his hand, and the pitcher stopped in flight. Similarly, Radomila was petrified on the spot, incapable of movement.

"Why don't you say that you got lost several times, that you are hungry and thirsty, that your hands and legs are scraped and tired? Why don't you ask for a pint of water and bread for dinner? I can't leave it like this; I would be sowing another seed of discontentment. You deserve punishment, and I will gladly undertake the task." He hiked up the princess's puffy skirt, which remained in the air as motionless as its owner.

"What is this supposed to be? What is it? Stop it immediately," fumed the little princess in surprise.

"You can talk for now, but if you continue to fume and curse, I will prevent you even that joy," calmly replied the wise man as he reached for his magic wand.

It was a pliable young twig. He swished it several times, making sure of its qualities. The little princess sensed trouble and tried to get loose from her invisible cuffs. However, she soon turned her attention elsewhere when the twig greeted her snow-white royal bottom for the first time.

Immediately a second stripe appeared nicely under the first one. Radomila was screaming her head off, but on her bottom, other colored lines appeared regularly, magically changing color from red to violet. Similarly, her tiny voice changed octaves. But the magic old man was used to his work, so he didn't heed swearwords, tears, promises, or the girl's crying.

He kept his promise to the king, putting the princess's mind right. Twenty-five stripes and welts decorated the bottom of tearful

Radomila, who, when the magic was over, slumped on the floor and cried bitterly.

"Radomila, go and kneel down on a pea in the corner. When you understand why you got your beating today, you may go to bed. Your things are already there." The old man sat down in an armchair again and appraised his work. The girl's striped behind was lovely. He was content. Radomila cried, but not a bad word she threw in. The fear didn't allow her to.

"May I go to bed already?" she asked after a while, painfully wriggling on the pea.

"So tell me, why did you get the beating, you naughty girl?"

"That was for the mean words toward you and for my untruthfulness and reserve, old man," she answered softly. She forced herself to speak, but she was contented that she had managed to answer.

"Yes, yes, Radomila, you may go to bed." The old man smiled and also went to bed.

Morning came quickly. The sun smiled and welcomed the new day. However, Radomila did not see it and continued to sleep on her tummy. The magic old man would not leave it like that. After knocking on the door, he entered the cubby. With magic, he waved off the comforter, slid the pillow under the princess's pelvis, and slipped the nightdress up. Radomila was awake in no time. However, her little legs were stiff with magic and, her little hands couldn't move either. The old man was angry.

"Radomila, you don't give a damn about God's sun, and you laze about all day. However, a young birch has much diligence in itself; hopefully, it will give you some," the old man said. His hand was already building up its energy for the first swish with the broom.

Radomila's shout could have been heard out the window as her pained flesh tasted the soft hair of the beautiful tree. Her skin was changing color as the welts flooded with redness. Radomila's eyes filled with tears. She cried and begged. She was ready to get out of bed right away if her behind could escape the new dolor. But the old man continued until he contentedly finished his work. Fifteen straight blows woke the girl to a new day.

"And now off to the corner and the pea with you." He sent the girl off crying and stroking her bottom, but the old man didn't loaf. He set tasks for her, such as dusting the room, beating the tablecloth, watering the flowers, cutting bread for breakfast, and washing the carrots.

When he allowed the young lady to get up, she quickly changed into a skirt and blouse, tied on a small apron, and started to do as he commanded. They had breakfast together before going down to the cowshed to clean, milk, feed, and otherwise care for the cows. The day ran at a quick pace, and after dinner, Radomila fell asleep.

As the days passed, Radomila learned politeness, diligence, and contentedness. She stopped demanding and began saying *please, thank you*, and *old man, may I*. The old man became more content, but he kept the magic twig ready to step in and put things right. Occasionally a few well-aimed swishes were needed, and once or twice he had her kneeling on the pea again.

Once, the little princess forgot cakes in the oven while she basked in the sun. The cottage filled with smoke, which made the magic old man angry. He woke Radomila up on the doorstep. She apologized immediately, but it was too late. Unhappily, and on the verge of tears, she looked at the ground. She knew her body would remember the burnt cakes for a long time.

The old man retrieved a wooden spoon from the cottage, and Radomila bent over his knees obediently, preferring to volunteer than to be forced with magic. She hiked up her skirt, and the old man started his admonition. Her bottom still remembered the first meeting with the twig and even the broom. Every blow smacked and slapped. The little princess cried and sobbed. She tried to protect herself with her hands, but the old man had more than enough strength to tame the fighting girl.

Ten days passed quickly, and the princess became homesick. She roamed the forest with the old man and furiously kicked a beautiful mushroom, which made the man very angry. However, he didn't say a word until they returned to the clearing. It was clear to Radomila that she was in for another thrashing. She started crying, knelt down, and begged the old man, "Please, please, don't beat me today. My bottom hurts so much! I will not handle another thrashing. I know I deserve it, but I will never kick any small mushroom again."

The old man didn't let her soften him up. He commanded the princess to lie down on the bench and hike up her skirt. Her bottom was full of colors.. The old man wasn't a brute, so he chose her youthful thighs as his target. The twig swished through the air, and the little princess shouted out. As the old man raised his hand for the second blow, Radomila shrieked and cried. Silently, she was thankful he wasn't beating her bottom. Nothing impeded the third swish. She was kicking her legs, but she didn't dare stand up.

After nine sharp swishes, the old man said, "Off to the pea with you. You got what you deserved." The weeping princess humbly went down on her knees with her skirt hiked up.

When her tears stopped, he allowed Radomila to stand up, and they prepared dinner. At bedtime, Radomila buried her head in her pillow and cried. The old man came to her to spread the welts with a healing salve and marveled at her grief. He knew it couldn't all be from the pain in her backside. So he asked, "What grief and sorrow have you on your mind?"

"I'm homesick, old man. I know you said you would let me go when you say I can go, and I know I wasn't very good today, but still, I'm asking you …" She began to cry again.

"Magic old man, please show me the way." She was sobbing. "Allow me to leave." She was crying. "I miss my daddy and mommy. I miss my horse. I will be a good girl." She looked really unhappy.

"Well, a good girl, but will you be content with your young life and all its beauties?"

"I will, really I will, old man; I promise."

"I'm not sure, Radomila; really I'm not sure. You were very insolent with your father, you were naughty to your mother, you beat the horse, provoked the guards, bullied your subordinates …" He named each of her transgressions and shook his head. The tearful princess got under the comforter and continued crying. The magic old man smiled and contentedly went away.

In the morning, Radomila got up with the lark, made breakfast, and waited for the old man. When they greeted each other, she cast down her eyes, which were still red from crying. The old man knew that the girl was reformed. Right after breakfast, he let her leave the clearing. As a keepsake, he gave her one pea and kissed her forehead.

"Hopefully, you have found contentment, child." He said good-bye to the reformed beauty.

As she rode off, Radomila looked back for the last time, hoping to wave her hand in greeting to the magic old man, but neither the cottage, nor the magical old man, were in the clearing anymore. The reformed princess set out toward the rising sun, and soon she set foot on the main road home.

Chapter Two

ICQ

Monick: Are you here?

Swish: Yeah, I am. What are you doing here?

Monick: I've just had lunch and don't feel like doing anything. I am just relaxing.

Swish: How are you doing?

Monick: Not bad. It's a bind at work now; plenty of work to do, and the chief is morose. Thank God he is in the office right now and doesn't annoy me. And what about you? Did you get it?

Swish: I also don't feel like doing anything. We start working on a new project, and that is always demanding. Yep, got it, yesterday. I went to the post office to get her. She is beautiful; smells of wood, firm but flexible. There is a nicely carved handle that enlarges a bit at the end to fit well … You would like it :-)

Monick: No doubt about that … ha. Do you think I would deserve any punishment?

Swish: Since you are using ICQ at work, definitely. :-)

Monick: Hm, you are probably right. I really shouldn't be doing that, for sure. Break the rules and the dry-as-dust chief would for sure keep my bonus. :-)

Swish: I would snatch off something else of you … Or rather take off slowly … A skirt? Pants?

Monick: Today, I have black pants on and under them … that you would take off too?

Swish: You can have anything under them; I would also take them off slowly and leave them lying at your feet. With lace? Or soft cotton clinging to you?

Monick: Dark purple, lace only along the edges, otherwise pure cotton, but I don't know how much longer since it's getting warmer in my lap ... :-) They are already lying at my feet, softly by my high heels. Is it OK like this?

Swish: No, no, I'm interested in the top too. All shapes must be appreciated ...

Monick: I'm unbuttoning my silky blouse slowly, button by button. We are getting closer to my breasts; the purple bra is flying away. Are you satisfied?

Swish: That's the way I like it. How would you like it today? Over the chair or by the table?

Monick: The table is big, and I can drape myself across it and enjoy every blow. I'm choosing the table ...

Swish: All right. Your body is appearing to me in its fullness, and not even your treasure stays hidden. I can hear your breath speeding up, full of expectation ... And what do you actually expect?

Monick: I'm waiting for the timeless moment when a new carved paddle travels through the air, and I'm trying to get ready for the moment ... For the moment when, for the first time, it touches my body and I, just for the sake of appearances, recoil. However, my senses revel in the lightly stinging pain and ache for more ...

Swish: It's getting nearer, building up energy and, for the first time, lands ...

Monick: Ach! I recoil and smile to myself ... More, please ...

Swish: Again, I'm holding out and smack to the other haunch ... It clicks nicely ...

Monick: Yes, my body crimps and immediately holds for another smack ... Please, keep on ... I want more, again and again. I want to experience this stinging pain that flies through my body ...

Swish: I will not spare you ... You will get five quick blows and ...

Monick: And with every blow I gently give a sigh. My body develops a red tinge ...

Swish: Now two and two from each side, but I intensify the
            acuteness. How does your pussy look?

Monick: *Ouch*, I painfully hiss—but the impact on my pussy is
            more than positive …

Swish: I'm glad to hear that; I'm not done yet. Now, slow but
            regular blows. I'm changing sides, and I'm savoring your
            pain … I will stop by number nineteen …

Monick: I'm savoring the pain with a tear in my eye and a moist
            lap. Slowly, I'm starting to waggle, and I feel a temptation
            to dodge, but I know that would make you angry.

Swish: Yes, for sure. Therefore, you are not going to do it. Instead
            of that, you accept six more there, where your thighs start,
            where it is sensitive.

Monick: You are … Ouch! It hurts nicely. That's already the end?
            That's a pity :-)

Monick: Swish, are you here?

"Yeah, I'm here." She heard a magisterial voice behind her.
Even the granite next to her seemed like a crumbling soft bread.

Oh my God, no! Monick thought to herself. *This is the worst
moment of my life; this is not possible. For a few weeks, I have been
chatting with Swish; we have never met; we just enjoy virtual
spanking—and the world is so terribly small that he is my boss! I'm
going to quit, right away; no one will see me here tomorrow! I'll move
away, to Europe, somewhere far away, where* no one *knows me. But
that means I have to pass him—no, I will not make it; I will sit here
until I take roots, or I will withdraw under a table, or … Gosh,
I wanna be invisible …*

"I've thought it was you for the last week, Monick …" he said,
already with a more lovely voice.

Monick: Why didn't you say anything?

She was still writing to chat, because she didn't have the strength
to look at him. He gazed over her shoulder and read.

"I wasn't certain, but today's dry-as-dust and a new project
assured me …" His tone was strict.

Monick: Ahem, what to say … Sir, I, I apologize. I will finish my
            work today …

"Of course, you will be here today overtime, but for another reason entirely. Monick, today it will not be only virtual; you will experience it in reality. And the 'Sir' that you use—you will not save the situation like this."

He gave the verdict, and with a totally professional look, he took a first bumf from a shelf—and without drawing any suspicion, he returned to his office. Then it showed on Monica's screen that Swish had gone offline.

She sat without any movement for another couple of minutes and tried to get her brain working again. Of course, for the rest of the day, she didn't really do anything; she spent the time absorbed in her thoughts. She didn't even leave her office, just went quickly to the bathroom and splashed water on her face before the end of the working day and the beginning … The beginning of an unexpected evening. Was there any possible way to avoid the evening? But wasn't this what she had always dreamed of, and found for it only a friend to talk to?

She felt an enormous fear and even greater excitement when he knocked on the door of her office. It was already half an hour after the end of work, and the office was empty …

"Come in," she answered, in the most relaxed tone that she could manage.

"Good evening, Monick."

"Good evening, sir." His mild coughing reminded her—"I mean, Swish."

"Come to my office," he spoke strictly but not angrily; he commanded respect but not fear. She was entranced by him; the whole situation totally amazed her.

In his office, he locked the door. She noticed *it* immediately when they walked in. *It* lay on the clean and almost empty table, on the red silken scarf. Really beautiful, just as he had described it. She couldn't keep from smiling. She faced the table and examined the tool of her punishment. *He must have gone home for it*, she realized.

"How do you want it today, Monick?" he asked. "The table, as in the afternoon?"

She had played the game already for a long time.

"Yes, I can lie down on it and enjoy the paddling," she answered quietly.

He smiled and walked very close up to her. He could smell the scent of her hair. He felt her shiver when he smelled it.

"Button by button …" he began.

She began slowly unbuttoning her blouse. Softly, he took it off and threw it away to the chair.

"What is hidden under the black pants?"

Slowly, she loosened her pants, letting them fall around her high heels and, carefully, stepped out of them. He picked them up and threw them at the chair.

"Even the top shapes must be appreciated." He slowly unfastened her bra and threw it at the chair.

"It's already lying underfoot." She was pulling down her panties.

They didn't have to speak more; they both knew what the other wanted.

He caressed her bottom and pushed her back; she elegantly lay down on the table, right next to the paddle. There was no boss and his inferior; there was Swish and Monick.

He tied up her braid with a scarf—she liked it like that—and firmly took the paddle into his hands.

"What do you expect?" he asked.

Her heart was thumping. She had a lump in her throat from fear and excitement.

"I'm waiting for the timeless moment when it will happen—when, for the first time, I will feel it on my body. I have fear."

"Enjoy it," he whispered in her ear, and a moment became an eternity. The paddle set out for her first, straight for its beautiful target. *Smack!* Monick lightly arched and delightfully breathed out. It was exactly as gorgeous as she expected. He gave her time to absorb it.

"Please, go on," she begged and held her bottom up for another blow.

Three more blows were given, and Monick went through her dream. Under the paddling, her rounded bottom flushed to the same color as her cheeks when her boss had showed up behind her in the office. Her mind focused only on the moment—the moment of each new blow. Her senses hungered for another stinging experience. Her pussy wanted more. It was much better than could have been described while chatting. After the fifteenth blow, her delightful sighs started to mingle with quiet sobs, but as Swish had said, she did enjoy it. The end was approaching—and he did what he had written; the last six blows to the sensitive place that always earns at least a small *ouch*.

She stayed bent over the table and breathed deeply after her first real spanking experience. She felt lighter … empty … calm.

"Are you all right?" Swish asked after a while.

"Yes … yes. I'm—I … It was fantastic. Oh, thank you, Swish." She straightened up slowly. Still, she didn't have the courage to look into his eyes. He did it for her. He turned her to his face and tenderly lifted up her head. His look was like an endearment. It wasn't her straightforward and hard boss, but a caring man. He kissed her on the forehead.

"Get dressed. We will talk about your working morale during dinner." He smiled foxily.

Chapter Three

Bodyguard

I've had enough; a man has only so much patience.
I'd gotten used to the fact that she constantly behaves like a brat, but today was the last straw. Ever since this morning, she'd been unpleasant, impudent, and rude to everyone, even though her team was working well, as usual, to work everything out. She yelled at hotel employees at breakfast; she threw glasses at them because the coffee was too hot. She swore at a bunch of children who wanted her autograph. When some stupid nitwit threw a firework at the stage and I acted—I knocked her down because of the suspicion of shooting—she told me to piss off. When the concert was over, we got a severe telling-off for incompetence, even though everything went according to plan and the concert turned out well; the audience asked again and again for the encore.

I was a bodyguard of this young hussy, and now I had an urge to do something. I didn't care how it ended up. I knew of two agencies that would employ me right away, so I didn't fear for the job at all; actually, I had nothing to lose.

We lived in the same apartment, which was advantageous, partly financially but especially with regard to safety; I was close by, in case something happened.

I entered her room without knocking. As I led her by the hand toward the bed, I let off the steam: "It was the high point of today; I should have done this a long time ago. You get on my nerves." I put her over my knee and, with no problem, hiked up her miniskirt, so that her young bottom stuck out at me in her close-fitting panties.

Her father had enough money; he had paid for a music teacher for his daughter, and afterward also her first concerts, then the realization team, and me. She was his only daughter—her mother had left them—so he spoiled his Lily ... but we cannot speak about a good upbringing.

"I should have done it a long time ago," I continued, while she swore and struggled. I made use of my self-defense training to catch her with my leg and pin one hand behind her back, so her second was good for nothing.

I had never heard as many swear-words as she showered me with when I started the spanking, but I just smiled and enjoyed our last meeting. In two minutes after I finished the spanking, I knew that her father was going to call and fire me; one more reason to enjoy it.

I had a firm hand and enough reasons for every spank, so soon her butt started to turn pink. She blustered, cursed, tried to slip out of my grasp—but to no avail. As I continued, she slowly began to sob, and, in the end, the first tears appeared. She was no longer fidgeting, because she realized that it wasn't worth doing it.

"That's enough! Stop it! It hurts! Leave me alone!" she begged among her sobs, after maybe thirty spanks.

But I absolutely wasn't planning on stopping it. Actually, it occurred to me that I hadn't heard the "magic word" from her for a long time—or maybe never? Hard to say. So I continued with the spanking and waited for her supplication. I gave her at least twenty more smacks before she added the magic word, amid her sobbing, to save the situation—and not just once but many more times she gave my ear this pleasure, so then I stopped spanking and let her go.

"You'll pay for this, you bastard!" she yelled at me, bawling. "My father will sack you, and you'll have to go sweep sidewalks, you fucker," she continued.

I put on a look as though nothing had happened. *Adios, you hoyden*, I thought. *I won't miss you ... Or will I?*

Suddenly it came to me; I held the ace in my hand.

As she reached for her cell phone, about to call her father, I took her by the hand and calmly warned her, "Call your father because your bodyguard has given you a good beating as if you were a little girl. Then I will tell him how his nice little girl carries a tiny bag of weed in her luggage."

Her eyes darted a sharp look at me. If her father ever found out about her marijuana habit, he would stop financing all of her concerts and her career as a singer. She knew that she would pay dearly for coming forward about the spanking ...

We sized each other up, and she gasped as she let her cell phone fall to the duvet.

"Yeah—and by the way, for that you will get more tomorrow. And before you say anything," I added quickly when she took a breath, clearly about to shower me with curses, "it's five more slaps for every swear word."

I turned away and left.

The following day went by as in a quiet household; the only words we exchanged were *good morning*, as a warning to her, that to wonder whether to greet me or not was pointless in her situation.

Giving autographs, taking pictures, and interviews passed off smoothly. In the evening, we met in her room. I was thinking of how to start today's spanking, when my phone rang. It was her father—playing right into my hands.

"Lily, your dad is calling. He heard that yesterday you were a bit *livelier* than usual. He wants to know if everything is okay." I gave her the cell phone, with a malicious smile.

"Hi, Poppa … Of course everything is okay … Yeah, I was having a whale of a time … Some glass; I will get someone to pay for it … Yeah, this—well, some fan threw a firecracker on the stage; otherwise nothing … Yeah, well, the bodyguard—yes, he did a great job; he protected me."

Her hateful look was aimed straight at me. I was standing in the door and waited with a calm smile, to see whether she was going to tell on me.

"Me too, Poppa. Good night." She folded up the phone and glared at me. "You fucker."

"That's five more."

I dodged the flying phone that smashed to pieces against the wall.

"And that's ten more." I held my ground, over the pieces of my phone.

"Poppa will surely buy you a new one since you saved his daughter from fans," she spluttered.

"Take your pants off—and try not to resist; forty is quite enough," I warned her, with a stern glance.

"Wow, Master is able to count."

"Don't worry; I will teach you that, and you will count every spank by yourself," I hit back.

Her sense of reason won, and she did what I wanted. She bent forward by the bed and put her hands on the mattress at my command.

The first ten minutes, I spanked her with a hairbrush from her bathroom; that was just for warming up. Every blow was accompanied by a soft hiss and a number. Her bottom turned nicely red. It was a just pity that after yesterday, it had lost its color.

I gave her some time and left to get a belt. By number twenty, she had tears in her eyes, and the pauses between blows were obviously longer. But she was filled with pride, and she didn't whimper for compassion. She waggled and shied her bottom away, but every deserved spank found its place. Slowly, dark red and, in several places, purple started to appear.

While I went for a bamboo sprig that stood in a pot in the other room, she started to sob fully. When I flicked it into the air, she straightened with fear, and with tearful eyes she asked me for lenience. But my eyes were uncompromising.

"You are getting just what you deserve. Lie down on the bed and put a pillow under your pelvis." I spoke calmly but authoritatively.

Her protective cover as a fearless and emancipated girl was lost. It was an ordinary girl with a sore behind and fear of another spanking who lay on the bed. No glare of spotlights and applause, no glittery clothes or fat bank account—just she herself. She was cute. I liked her like this, natural, plain, with no affectation, honest to herself. It was a shame that it had to be under such circumstances.

She screamed number twenty-one together with *ouch*, when I first flicked her with the bamboo sprig. In spite of it, she remembered to stay lying down. The fear of more punishment was, after all, stronger than the sharp pain that was going through her body. Then, three more blows came, and every flick was accompanied by crying. I eased up the intensity, because I didn't want to hurt her. It was clear to me that her bottom had become much more tender after the previous series.

By number thirty, she couldn't stand it any longer. "Jeremy, please, that's enough ... It hurts too much ... No more..."

"There are ten more left for the broken cell phone," I reminded her.

Her crying grew more intense. "I'm sorry; I went too far ... Forgive me. It won't happen again—honestly," she started to beseech and promise. Maybe I would even believe her, but I intended to finish the punishment.

I told her to bend over my knee, and the rest I gave her just by hand. I may even have caught a glimpse of thankfulness under the flood of tears.

When I was done, I helped Lily to stand up and let her cry next to the bed. I left for my room and just quietly warned her to watch her behavior tomorrow.

I wept far into the night. The pain was slowly easing, and a cold towel helped.

How dare he do this?

He had been my bodyguard for three years, and he had always been a polite and straightforward man. He always knew what to do, and he was able to ensure my security even during unexpected situations at concerts. I was in a fury. Well, true, straightforward he was, today and also yesterday, and polite actually too—he even knew what to do with me—but he had given me a good beating and that was not allowed.

But why do I slowly cease to be angry at him and find that I'm more angry at myself? Was I really so terrible that I'd forced him to risk his job and reputation when he decided to give me a good talking-to?

In these and similar thoughts, I finally fell asleep.

In the morning, his gentle voice woke me up. "Lily, get up; we have to catch the plane."

When I came into the room to have breakfast, there was juice and muesli prepared for me as usual. Only a soft pillow on the chair was a nice surprise. With a glance I thanked him for this kindness. Still, I didn't sit comfortably, and Jeremy left for the bedroom smiling rather than trying to keep a neutral face.

After I'd packed up, he helped me with my luggage into the taxi and up to the airport. In the airplane, he brought me a blanket and inconspicuously, with an insignificant look, he gave me a pillow under it. But still, the three hours in the airplane felt to me like sitting on glass shards for a week.

Our quiet work continued. Somehow I didn't know how to face this situation. Either to hate him for the physical attack—or how could I call spanking professionally?—or to admire him for his directness and attempt to do something. Should I despise him for the medieval practices of punishment for women or kiss him for doing me a security service—protection not only of my body against attacks of madmen but also protection of me myself against bossy, impudent, vulgar, and other bad behavior that would gradually get more and more under my skin til I became the most unpleasant celebrity in the world, hated by all her employees?

The next two weeks passed with slow sessions of CD recording and casual small actions for charity and press, so everything was all right. I didn't need Jeremy's assistance very often, and when he was guarding me I ignored him, with a distant look. He did his job, and I did mine. I gave him no reason for another spanking; I treated him formally, and I choose the right words when talking to my team. But … I did miss him …

A text message beeped: *What kind of bodyguard are you, when you don't know about my secret rented apartment?*

I smiled. So the princess had awoken from her offended dream.

Do you mean St. Godfrey Street 145/95, the roof apartment?

Of course I knew about it; it was my job. She leased it under the name of a friend.

I expect you here within an hour; I have a problem, was the answer.

Damn! I had wanted to go bowling with a friend of mine. I called it off, took a taxi to get to her street, and walked the rest of the way.

"Hi, Jeremy," she greeted me amiably.

I pretended that I was coming because of business, that I didn't notice that she came to open the door in a satin bathrobe. There was a bottle of champagne and two glasses and a dish of strawberries on the table—and a brush and a pillow waiting on the sofa.

Does she really feel the same attraction? So many times in the last two weeks, I had thought of her, so many times I'd imagined kissing her tears away after a spanking, and soothing her; many times, I just wanted to hold her hands. I was falling in love with my client.

"Maybe I was lying a bit when I wrote you that I have a problem. You know, I …"

"So, what is it? And don't tell me 'nothing'; that would make me angry. I canceled bowling with my friend because of you." I tormented her with steely nerves and a bit of a laugh.

"I … You know … Why are you making this so hard?" she asked, sadly.

"Because you deserve it," I said strongly.

"I missed you. I wanted to see you—not only as a bodyguard but as a man … That's why I asked you to come."

She spoke quietly and stared at me with her gentle girly look that I didn't see very often. She wasn't the virago on the stage and the hellcat offstage; I was surprised.

"You opened my eyes by those spankings, and I see myself in a different light. I feel bad about my behavior. I feel ashamed. I … I've never thanked you for your work; I've never really valued it. I always felt comfortable with you. I ... fell I love with you. Could today be our first date? ... Please, say something."

"So you lied to me about having a problem? You deserve a punishment for that," I answered, already smiling. "And the date that we are going to have after spanking? On a first date, I don't give a woman a beating, on principle." I winked at her.

She cast down her gaze, and with a smile, she came to me on the sofa. She knelt in front of me, kissed me, lay down on my lap, and put her behind out.

"So, it isn't possible like this, Lily." I took off her purple and white lace panties. "Well, that's better."

I started to stroke her behind with one hand, and with the other, from time to time, I smacked her with the brush. Her hisses sounded more like sighs, and soon she was purring in my lap like a kitten. After twenty-five soft smacks, I gave her rosy bum a stroke, kissed it, and carried my hoyden away into the bedroom.

Chapter Four

A Different View

I never understood why she didn't use a shower curtain while taking a bath. She said she would rather wipe the floor than be like in a "Hitchcock" movie. I have no idea what that meant, but probably he used to take a bath and use a shower curtain, and it was nothing to shout about. She was really beautiful; I liked her curves a lot.

Slowly she undressed and got into the bath, hung the hose on the wall, and began to enjoy the first drops of the hot water. They trickled down her soft skin. That it was soft, I knew definitely. I made sure of it several times each night. It was kind of my secret; she didn't know about it.

Her long hair merged into one strand, which meandered down her back. She started to stroke her breasts with one hand, and with the other she fondled her face, but slowly it went lower and lower, to the very bottom there. Her fingers started to play between her legs, and she closed her eyes with delight.

Suddenly, her body bent as if she had gotten a stroke with a cane. Oh yes, why hadn't it occurred to me? And now again, again, the back-bend under an imaginary swish, and the forefinger disappeared somewhere inside her. Her husband is on his business trip, so for sure she pleasured herself while thinking of that recent night …

I was in the kitchen when Martin got home. Right in the doorway she kicked up a fuss, like where had he been hanging around, and that she'd had to go shopping without his car, and that he should make dinner himself because she had a movie going on … Martin knew that it was just an ordinary provocation and that she didn't mean anything serious by it, but still, this, her game, always made him angry. It made him angry just a bit, just enough to not be shy, but to take a cane from the wardrobe and welcome his nice wife as she was asking for.

He took off his jacket and tie, and commanded her to undress and bend down over the bed. I had to put a bit of effort into moving away, but I managed it just in time as the first stroke landed and Jane's bottom was decorated with its first red stripe.

My experienced eyes recognized that today, Martin was sparing her. And as I found out later, my suspicion that he wanted to give her more blows than usual, was true.

The pleasant swish was the herald of already less pleasant blows on the naked bottom of Jane the inciter—which, thanks to its decoration, was starting to look like some kind of creature that I had spotted once on television. A zebra, or something like that.

Jane carried on bravely; after every blow she hissed and nicely bent backward, or she escaped with her bottom forward. Martin didn't hurry; he enjoyed every blow and aimed with deliberation. The sensual suspense in the room was thick enough to cut with a knife. Martin's pants were starting to get tight, and a mysterious droplet rolled down Jane's thigh. Soon her first teardrops started to fall onto the mattress, and I heard a sigh of relief as the twenty-fifth blow struck.

What a great surprise when the twenty-sixth blow landed.

"Martin, what the …? Not this, no more, please! This really hurts!" she started to beg tearfully.

Twenty-seven …

"Really?" asked her husband, as if it was something that he couldn't believe. "You had enough verve just a while ago, when you barked at me," he warned her.

Twenty-eight …

"Ouch! I admit it, I went a bit too far. Please stop; I apologize," she chose diplomatic words amid her tears.

"So are you going to be a kind wife now, with plenty of nice words for your husband?" he asked, as if he were some respectable professor.

Twenty-nine …

"*Ouch!* Yes, I'm going to. Stop, please …"

"And are you even going to prepare us something good for supper?" Martin wasn't put off so easily.

Thirty …

"Yes, I will! But this really hurts," she begged.

He knew that she was used to more intense blows but in smaller numbers. The suspense at around number twenty-one had started to make her very nervous—and excited? A small lesson of uncertainty couldn't hurt.

Thirty-one …

"And are we going to make love tonight?" another question, as if it were a game of *Truth or Dare*.

She smiled between sobs. "Yes," she breathed.

Thirty-two ...

The last wave of pain, that last evasive move of her bottom; after that I saw only two entwined bodies whispering tender words. It was nice of him to finish at a multiple of the number of my eyes, with which I was watching them curiously.

Later in the evening, after supper—which, of course, she'd had ready in the fridge in advance—Jane smiled happily, snuggled down in the arms of her husband, and blissfully fell into the realm of dreams ...

The hot water intensified her arousal, and the memories brought her closer to the climax. In strange muscle cramps, with fingers scratching a wall tile running with condensation and with a hand expertly working in her lap, she was rising on the waves of pleasure. Then, for a while longer, she enjoyed a warm shower before she got out in front of the mirror and started to dry herself.

Before she hit me with a towel and I left my cobweb forever, I managed to wish to be born as the woman of some nice man in my next incarnation. Or the man of some nice woman ...

Chapter Five

An Examination Period

My name is Martina, and I study at the Faculty of Economics and Administration in Brno. I live in the dormitory with my friend Susan. Once, before the examination period, when we were talking with our friends Lenka and Clara about what could have an influence on better study results, thrashings were mentioned, just for a joke.

Susan said, "When I was a small girl, I would get a good beating from my mom for every failed exam, and I would definitely try harder." Then we talked for a while about how we, as little girls, used to get thrashings. It emerged that we all, from time to time, had gotten a beating from our parents—most often with a hand, but also often with a wooden spoon. Sometimes Lenka got a thrashing by a belt, and Clara and her brother got a carpet beater several times for some major offenses. Thrashings proved to be a topic that we all liked, and we agreed on using thrashings for improvement of our study results.

We agreed to meet during the examination period on Thursdays at eight in our room. Each of us would bring the credit book, and according to it we would evaluate how we studied. Always at least a week in advance we would write down in the exercise book which exams we planned to do in the next week and which credit tests we planned to take. That was in order to see even the postponement of the exam.

Of course, there would be no punishment for grades of A or B, and for the grade C just a light one. Real punishments would begin with the grade D, and the toughest punishments waited for us for failing the exam or the credit test.

We had to arrange what kind of punishment we would get for a worse grade or for failing the exam. We agreed that for a grade C there would be ten blows over our panties, for a D fifteen, for an E twenty, and for failing twenty-five on a naked bottom. We would determine the tool and position by rolling dice.

We also agreed straightaway what kinds of tools we would get ready for next Thursday. Before that, there was a difficult exam in microeconomics waiting for us.

Microeconomics was really hard and turned out badly. When we met at eight in our room and locked the door so no one would disturb us, we knew that three of us would experience the thrashing for the first time. Lenka would go unpunished because she got a B. It would be worse for Susan, who got a grade D; there would be fifteen blows landing on her naked bottom. Worst of all for me and Clara because, unfortunately, we didn't pass the exam, and so in a little while, each of us would be given twenty-five on our naked bottoms.

I am worried, expecting what was going to happen next, and I curse my decision to take part in this game.

First we put the tools on the table from which we would draw lots. On the table there appeared a big wooden spoon, a long wooden ruler, a leather belt, a hazel switch, a wooden hairbrush, and a rubber hose. We numbered the tools from one to six.

We would also draw to decide the positions for the performance of the thrashing. For number one, we would have to bend over the edge of the table; number two meant bending over the back of the chair; number three, to lay down on the bed on our stomach; four, to kneel at the side of the chair; five, to kneel on the bed on all fours; and six, to lie down on our back on the bed and put our legs behind our head, as if doing a backward roll.

We sit at the table, gazing at the tools and thinking of which one of us will be the first.

"You will draw lots to decide in which order you will get a spanking," says Lenka, who is easy in her mind and is organizing it all today. "Each of you will throw the die, and you will get a thrashing in order from the lowest number to the highest one."

I was the first one to take the die and threw it. I threw a five; Clara threw a two and Susan a four. Clara will be the first one to get a thrashing—and she will get the highest punishment: twenty-five blows.

Lenka invites Clara to roll for her instrument. She throws a three, so she will get a thrashing with the belt.

"Now draw the position," Lenka orders. Clara draws the back of the chair.

Lenka commands Clara to get the chair ready. Clara takes the chair and places it in the middle of our room so that there is enough space from the side of the backrest.

"Clara, stand and face the backrest of the chair, undo your jeans, let them fall to the ground, and pull your underpants down to your knees," Lenka commands.

Clara follows her instructions, and soon she is standing with her bare bottom in front of the chair, ready for the thrashing. Clara has long black hair, blue-green eyes, and a tall, slim, athletic figure. Her bottom is small, but firm and nicely rounded. So far, her skin is all light pink—but its color will turn red soon.

"So now stand close to the chair and bend over the backrest! According to the rules, you will get twenty-five with the belt. You, alone, will count them aloud," Lenka informs her about the punishment.

Clara stands obediently, bent over the chair, with her bottom naked and exposed, worrying about what is going to happen next.

Lenka takes the belt into her hand and folds it in the middle. She comes toward Clara, raising her hand for the first blow.

The first blow lands on Clara's bare behind. Both her bare buttocks shiver, and Clara shrieks, "One!"

Lenka is raising her hand for the second blow. On Clara's exposed bottom blows of the belt land at regular intervals, and Clara carefully counts them aloud in front of us. Her behind turns red quickly. Halfway through the punishment, after thirteen blows, Lenka takes a short pause, but soon she raises her hand for another blow.

After the twenty-five blows, Clara's bottom is totally red, and Lenka allows her to leave her position by the chair.

Clara slips quickly into her panties and jeans, which are lying on the floor, and pushes the chair back up to the table. So Clara has her thrashing behind her. Now it's Susan's turn.

Susan throws the dice twice to draw the tool and the position for her thrashing. Lenka announces her punishment right away: "You will get fifteen blows with the spoon, on the bed with your legs behind your head. So get ready for the thrashing! Take off your clothes from the waist down, and lie down on the bed."

Susan stands up from the table, undoing her blue skirt, letting it fall to the floor, and pulling down her white underpants. She puts her skirt and underpants away on the chair. According to Lenka's instruction, Susan comes over to the bed and lies down on her back.

Susan is a blonde, with her hair cut short, blue eyes, and a petite figure. Lenka takes the big spoon from the table and comes to the bed, where Susan is lying ready for her punishment.

"Put your legs behind your head, and hold them with your hands under your knees!" Lenka commands.

Susan obediently puts up her legs, and we can see her totally bare, uncovered bottom—and also other intimate, completely shaved, areas of her body.

Lenka, with the spoon in her hand, steps closer to her, holding Susan's legs with her left hand, and raising the right one for the first blow. She warns Susan to count the blows carefully.

The first blow with the spoon lands on Susan's pretty, exposed bottom, and we all hear a strong smack. Susan counts: "One." Lenka raises her hand for the second blow, and the spoon lands again with a loud smack on Susan's bare buttocks. While Susan counts aloud, other blows follow, and her naked bottom turns red. After fifteen blows, it's pretty red.

Lenka lets Susan go; she can finally leave the unenviable position on the bed with her legs behind her head. She puts on her pants and skirt and sits at the table—even though she now has a little trouble sitting.

Now it's my turn. I can't say that I feel fine at all.

"Martina, now you draw," Lenka invites me. Obediently I take the die into my hand and throw it twice. I draw the rubber hose, in a kneeling position bent over the seat of the chair.

Lenka seizes the initiative right away, commanding me, "Martina, get the chair ready; you will get twenty-five spanks with the rubber hose!"

I don't want to do it, but I must; we arranged it like this. I take my chair and place it so that I can kneel beside the seat.

"Martina, take off your clothes from the waist down and kneel by the chair!" Lenka commands me. I undo my jeans and take them off. I pull my underpants down and put my clothes on the table. I walk to the chair and kneel on the floor from the side of the chair.

"Now bend over the seat," Lenka orders. "And count the blows carefully!"

I'm already kneeling, bent over the seat. My bare behind is ready for the rubber hose. I have no idea how much this will hurt, but I will find out soon.

Lenka takes the rubber hose from the table and stands above me. She raises her hand for the first blow. Subconsciously, I'm pressing my buttocks together, and soon a stinging pain goes through my body.

"One." I don't forget to count. It is going to be really terrible to stand twenty-five such blows.

Lenka raises her hand properly, and the rubber hose lands on my bottom for the second time. I feel like squealing with pain, but I can't show that I'm a namby-pamby. Instead of screaming, I say, "Two."

And so it goes on. I'm only thinking about how badly it stings. I'm holding the chair strongly and counting mechanically. The blows land on my thighs and ass at regular intervals. After thirteen blows, Lenka takes a short pause. I'm thankful for a moment of a rest.

But soon my suffering continues. The twenty-five blows seem endless. I'm sure my buttocks are totally red. I'm longing for the end.

Finally, Lenka puts the hose away, letting me leave my ignominious position by the chair.

Quickly I stand up and dress. When I put my underpants on, I can feel the hot skin of my buttocks.

Today's thrashing is over; we will meet again next week.

Chapter Six

A Punishment

"Next!" I call.

A girl comes in, unwillingly. She is young—can't be more than seventeen—and quite pretty, even though she sniffles, which kind of spoils the nice impression.

"So, what brings you here?" I ask. It's my little joke. There is only one thing that can bring them here.

And really—I can see guilt on her face. She feels bad.

And of course, fear. Guilt and fear: my two everlasting companions.

With a wave of my hand, I ask her to come to me. She doesn't want to, but she goes. She has no other choice.

She is shaking when she comes within reach, and I hike up her skirt. She feels weepy when her underpants—a weird fashion that the whites brought here—slide down and uncover her snow-white bottom. Without resistance, she lets me put her on the heavy woolen blanket that I have on my knees.

I ask her about her transgressions—they are nothing extraordinary; just common things. When I repeat them, she just nods and doesn't speak any more. At the moment, no one speaks. She will start to make sounds later, when my hands proceed to their assigned task. The space fills with the sounds of her weeping and the regular slapping with which naughty girls are punished.

It doesn't take too long. Soon the girl is leaving. With satisfaction, I see that I wasn't wrong—she pulls her underpants on, and with her hands, presses her burning buttocks together. She is too bashful. Some of them leave with naked bottoms and don't trouble about the fact that outside, some boys hoping to get a glimpse of something might lurk. I think that they used to be there. I myself have never seen them, though.

"Next!" I call.

The next girl who comes in is a bit of a surprise to me. "Nigili!" I say. "What are you doing here? It's not such a long time since you were here last."

"You know," she answers. "Things happen."

"But to you, it is happening a bit too often, don't you think?"

"Actually, I wanted to see you," she smiles.

"Me? No one wants to see me." But deep down, it quite pleases me. "But what have you actually done?" I want to know.

"Well ... I shoved Menbe into a river."

I nod. "Was he making advances to you?"

"Of course—it's Menbe."

"Many girls don't even take the trouble to come here because of him."

"Is it my fault that I have a sense of duty?" But we both know that there is something more to it.

Nigili is not dressed in style of the whites; she wears only a skirt made of grass. Carefully she takes it off, so it doesn't crease, and gladly lies down over my knee.

"Is there anything more I should know about?" I ask.

"Well, maybe about the twig ..."

"What twig?"

"My little sister took from somewhere a red twig. It wasn't of wood; I guess it must be one of the white things. I was in a hurry and stepped on it. It broke."

"And?"

"She cried. I'm really sorry," she sighs. "I think that I really do need to be punished for that."

I nod. "And that's it?"

"Yes ..." She shakes. "It's cold in here."

Yes, that it is. I'm used to it. But for those who are used to frolicking in the sun, the cave is really unpleasantly cold.

"I'm gonna warm you up," I say, and start thrashing her.

In surprise, she let out a shriek. But soon, her noises change into crying. I concentrate on my work.

While she is getting dressed, she asks: "Why don't you ever go out?"

I just smile. "You know that it's not possible. And why would I? Do I not have everything that I need in here? "

"The others said that you can't—but why?"

"You are still young," I smile. "Too young for me to tell you." I reach out and lightly smack her sweet behind. "Curiosity doesn't pay, you know?"

"I want you to come out sometime," she says. "I would show you the village. It must have changed a lot, for sure."

I don't answer.

"Next!" I call, to show her that our meeting is over.

Some time later, Nigili visits me again. Has it been a week? A month? A year? I have no idea. But it probably wasn't too long. Menbe still doesn't want to leave her alone. And she will finally succumb to him; I know it, Menbe knows it, finally she knows it too, but she still teases him.

Menbe isn't that bad. From the village gossips that I overhear, I know that soon his children will be born. Hopefully there will be some boys among them. There are just five young boys in the village; the girls exceed them more than five times over. I have a vague memory that it wasn't always like this. Or is just my memory deceiving me? That is also one of the reasons why girls come to me; everyone thinks highly of the boys—even though from time to time, they behave really unbearably.

Nigili tells me of her experiences with Menbe, and I smile. She smiles too, despite the fact that she is lying bent and knows that in a short time, I will color her bottom red.

"A white woman has come," Nigili mentions.

"Oh really?"

"She spoke to me. She takes an interest in you."

"In me? Why?"

"Supposedly, no other village is the same as ours," she announces proudly.

"That's probably true," I admit.

"She asked who is the oldest one. So we told her that it was you."

"That is certainly true," I agree. "But she can hardly come here."

"That I also told her," she smiles. "But listen—didn't we change the subject?"

"True," I smile and raise my hand. My thoughts about the mysterious white women are drowned by her screams.

"Next!" I call.

It's some time later. How much? Who knows? I don't count the time.

With surprise I watch a tall woman who is coming in. She must be the white woman—even though it seems that she is not that much paler than us. I can recognize her because her whole body is covered. Some girls told me that she must be terribly ugly, to cover her body this way—that she is all covered with sores and scabs, for sure. I didn't argue with them. They are young, and they have never known anything really different. Except for me.

Many of them think that the white woman is stupid, because she asks about things that must be clear to everybody. I know that we wouldn't be doing any better in her world. It's easier to consider others inferior rather than different. That's true for all people.

"Hello," the white woman says.

I nod. She has strange pronunciation. "What brings you here?" I ask.

"I wanted to talk to you."

"About what?"

"This is a very strange village. The people don't realize it, but I think that you do."

I nod. "Yes, it is strange."

"There are too few men and too many women. And this cave … Girls from the village go to you for …"

She hesitates. Was it just my imagination or did her face turn a bit darker? In the eternal half-light of the cave, I see quite well, but even I have some limits.

"For a thrashing," I nod. "Tell me, do you also do it in your land? In mysterious Europe?"

"Yes." She smiles a bit. "But not at such a scale. Parents punish their children, usually."

"Here, parents leave it to me."

"You never leave the cave?"

"I can't."

"Why not?"

I close my eyes. "What have you done?" I ask.

"Excuse me?"

"You are here. You know why girls come here. Everyone has some transgression. What is yours?"

"Is it so strange to think that I just wanted to talk to you?" She sounds offended.

"No." I shake my head. "You want answers, and you've found out already that no one else will give you them. But that doesn't alter the fact that people come into this cave only for one purpose."

"How long have you been here?"

"Does it matter?"

"It matters to me. People from the village don't remember the time when you weren't here. And some of them are older. Sixty, seventy years. But you don't look old."

"I ... I'm not like them," I admit.

"So what kind of person are you?"

"What is your transgression?" I ask again. "If you want to know my secrets, you must tell me yours."

She pauses in thought. "I really can't think of anything."

I nod. "Can I touch your hand?"

She hesitates for a moment. "Well ... all right." She holds out her hand, and I take it into mine.

I close my eyes. "Being far away from your home worries you. You live with a man—you've left your child with him to come here, but the thought that it was selfish worries you. That is the feeling of guilt."

She recoils. "How ... how do you know this?"

"There is a reason why girls would rather tell me everything," I smile.

"You have been sitting in this cave for decades ... thrashing young girls. Isn't it now your turn to tell me who you are?"

"I'm not totally sure," I say, with consideration, "but I think that I'm god."

"God?"

"There was a time when I was young. It was a very, very long time ago. I used to be a shaman of our village, and I talked with the gods. Already back then, I liked to thrash young girls. As a shaman, I had many opportunities for that; I knew about their transgressions and punished them for them. But while I was responsible for the village and lived with consequences of my decisions, the gods didn't. They did what they wanted, and berating them was of no avail.

"I had a wife back then, you know? She became ill and passed away. All my knowledge was for nothing. I begged the gods for help, but they didn't help me. I heard them laughing. I wanted to be like them—so I wouldn't have to look after anything. And they made my wish come true. How much were they laughing then!"

I reach for the heavy blanket on my knees and push it away. In the eyes of the white woman I see a gleam of horror. My thighs begin brown, like any human, but their bottom part is stone, grown together with the stone seat on which I sit. On which I have sat for centuries and thrashed girls upon that part of the body which I myself don't have.

"I don't eat, and I don't drink," I continue quietly, "and still I don't get older. I live on. I'm not answerable to anyone—still just doing what I loved as a human. And because I like to thrash girls so much, the village is full of them ... full of naughty girls who will never grow totally, and just as many young men, so another generation can be saved. The gods are able to do this to a person. Funny, don't you think?"

I put the heavy blanket back. "I don't show this to everyone," I tell her. "Most of the girls don't think about me very much ... From time to time, they come to me, and then try to push me out of their heads. Sometimes I think about what the gods actually wanted to do ... Is this my reward or my punishment?"

The white woman is stupefied. Her bottom is trapped in a close-fitting cloth undergarment, but when I undo it on the front and start pulling down, she doesn't resist. I have never seen such clothes before, but I know what to do with it. One of the unusual abilities of my position.

"So now you will punish me?" she asks me when I lay her on the heavy blanket. "Is it really so bad to want to achieve something or to find things out?"

"No, it's not." I shake my head. "But you think so. It's visible. You left your child, and even though you believe that the thing you will get is worth the separation, you can't fully persuade yourself of it."

"You're right," she says, hesitantly. She jerks when my fingers go down to her underpants, but obediently she lets me to pull them down.

I nod, just to myself, when I don't see any sores or scabs on her behind. Not that I believed it, but it's good to be sure.

Then, the smacking starts. She is strong, more resistant than the village girls, but not even she tolerates it too long.

I hold her on my knees, which will never let me rise again, waiting till she has had a good cry. I can see into her soul; she needed a pretext. There are so many pictures, so many things that I don't understand, but I know that not everything in her life was happy. But she has been too shy to cry; her people think it's an expression of weakness. That's a mistake. I hold her on my knees and let her weep the years of tears that have accumulated in her.

"How do you feel?" I ask her at last, when she has no more tears.

She doesn't answer, but I know it. She feels relief. Her feeling of guilt is gone, drained off with tears. She stands up and gives me a hug—surprising herself.

"Meeting me will certainly look good in your travelog," I say.

"I ... I don't think that I will mention this village in it. Not even you. No one would believe me."

"I'm not going anywhere," I interpose "You could persuade them—if you really wanted to."

She nods. "Yes, I could ... but maybe I will first try to find out more. Sometime I would like to come back here."

"You will be welcome," I nod.

She pulls her underpants on, but the cloth that fits so closely over her legs and behind is too much for her. She throws the garment across her hand and leaves. At least she can disprove a myth, which I haven't told her about.

She leaves the cave and I, the god of thrashings, who wasn't even allowed to be dissatisfied with my destiny, smile.

"Next!" I call.

Chapter Seven

Another Story from the Wild West

I have never complained about my life. I was taking it as it was coming. It gave me something but also took something, but that's just the way it is. I couldn't choose my destiny any more than I could have chosen the color of my hair, right?

I had been working as a prostitute—how nice it sounds—since I was about fifteen, when I first had to stand on my own two feet. My father drank himself to death, and my mother went off with another man. My sister married a rich man, and her husband took her far away from the town. She wasn't allowed to tell me where she was going, much less to take me with. No one cared about me. How many opportunities does such a pretty young girl have, alone in the Wild West? Exactly—just one.

I started on my own in the street, but even there, one can meet nice people, if I may put it this way. Under the so-called care of my pimp, who kept me in near-slavery, I at least got under a roof, and in the warmth of my room I gave others a pleasure. There were more than enough stinking drunkards and brutes touching my body. A person becomes apathetic and thinks only of money, money—which is never enough to get you out of that life; the pimps see to that.

I wasn't naïve; I didn't expect that I would find happiness there. I didn't expect it, and certainly not with the drunken bumptious old buffer who thought that he was allowed to do anything he wanted with me …

"You bitch, I said shut up," he yelled at me.

I jumped, crying out, as he swished me strongly with a belt. I could feel drops of blood running down my thigh. This was going too far. I was used to the fact that from time to time, someone would beat me up and get off on it, but to let somebody damage my tool for work—that I definitely would not allow.

"You think you can beat me bloody, you old boozer? Piss off!" I spat in his face.

A hard slap to my cheek clouded my sight, and the light returned to me only as I was getting up from the ground. I felt the salt taste of blood in my mouth. Quickly I stood up and ran out of the room.

By the banister above the salon, I started crying for help. But the man seized my hair and tried to yank me back into the room. I struggled and kicked his … exactly that. He raised his hand and whipped me with the belt across my back. I shrieked and hoped for someone to help me. It was an unwritten rule in this town that prostitutes asking for help would receive assistance.

Suddenly, all went quiet in my mind, because I was gaping into the barrel of the old drunk's pistol. The click of the hammer echoed in my head, and I waited for the roar of the shot that would end my dog's life. I had no regrets about anything; I was reconciled to departing my life. I closed my eyes. I imagined a beautiful meadow, with fresh green grass, and a young mare waiting for me to mount up and ride away. Yes, that would be a nice vision before departure, don't you think?

I heard a bang, but kind of hollow. I opened my eyes curiously and saw the old drunk tumbling down the stairs, still clutching his belt, and lay still, flat as a slice of bread, on the floor, surrounded by a few of his teeth.

In front of me, a male hand appeared and helped me to stand up. I realized that I was standing in front of my savior wearing only garters and a loosened corset. But his eyes filled me with a sense of peace; they were so deep and calm. They started to draw me into their depths, and I didn't resist. I was engulfed by the darkness.

I awoke in my room. The mysterious man was there with me, waiting for me to awaken. He helped me to my feet. We stood face to face and let the time fly in the moment of connection. Slowly we moved closer, until our bodies were almost touching. I could feel the warmth of his body and a calm breath.

"Why do you do it?" he asked mildly.

"I have no other choice," I answered.

"Are they at least nice to you?"

A more naive question I could not have imagined. Instead of answering, I smiled sarcastically.

"A woman is beautiful. She should be taken care of and not hurt." He was throwing out more pearls. He did not sound like a man from these times.

"I'm nothing to them, nothing. I satisfy their lust, and they won't even remember me the next day. If no one hits me for a whole day, that is a beautiful day." I tried to bring him back to reality.

He stroked my face and lightly kissed my cheek. "Have you ever experienced anything nice?"

"Nice? What do you mean *nice*? I only know it here; I'm doing it only with my clients."

He started untying my corset and freed my breasts. He was kissing my nape, my midriff, leaving me in only my garters. My "little cave" was exposed before him, and my soft, pale ass was bare.

Suddenly, he pulled a withe from his under pants leg. I stiffened. What was this supposed to be? He circled around and stood behind me. I felt how he lightly stroked my back with the withe, working his way down to my bottom.

"Bend over and hold your ankles," I heard his firm voice. There was no space for protesting. *Of course,* I thought, *another one of those brutes who pleasure themselves with one hand while they beat the daylights out of me with the other.*

My eyes filled with sorrowful tears, which trickled toward the ground. My bottom was at his mercy, the mercy of a stranger who had saved my life and now was asking for a reward.

I heard the withe cutting through the air, and then I felt only its mild impact. That was definitely not like the blows from the hands of those other brutes. A mild pain went through my body—and a pleasant surprise.

He stroked the pink stripe on my bottom and kissed it. He repeated this ten times, and then gently turned his attention to my "little shell," which had become damp and eager. He teased me pleasantly with his fingers and, from time to time, interspersed his stroking with a few swishes.

I had never expected that a thrashing could be so pleasurable, and I started to enjoy it. I repaid each blow with a delighted sigh and every stroke with a drop of love. Soon he took me from behind and finished his work on the bed, where we both achieved our goals.

We lay next to each other, and his deep eyes started to engulf me again. *No, I don't want to,* I thought. *Don't take my dream away. I don't want to wake up ...*

I was lying on my bed, in my room. I opened my eyes slowly, and met the dark gaze of my mystery man. I tried to smile, but my face hurt, thanks to the smack from that drunken brute. Gently, my savior applied a cooling compress to my cheek.

"Thank you," I said quietly, and held out my hand in greeting. He nodded subtly and was gone before I could blink.

Oh yeah, girl, welcome back to reality. The day off cost me money—and, strangely, a photograph had disappeared from my room after his rescue. The frame remained, but the picture was gone. My pimp was angry at the day of lost business and made it clear that everything I should have earned would be added to my debt to him—already enormous. The next day, I hid my previous experience under a layer of makeup and, with my body, welcomed nighttime clients.

After one especially busy night, I returned exhausted to my room in the morning. I closed the door and started to undress, looking forward to being alone in my bed. Suddenly, someone caught me around my waist from behind and covered my mouth.

"Don't scream; I don't want to hurt you." He let me go, and in the low light, I looked into his deep eyes. He turned on the lamp and showed me the picture that had disappeared along with him.

"Do you know this woman?" he was pointing to the brunette next to me, a small smiling girl holding a ball.

My eyes blurred, and I nodded. Of course that I knew her; she was my sister.

"She paid me to find you."

I started crying fully.

"We have no time," he continued. "I've bought supplies for the journey, and there's a horse waiting behind the building. We have to set out quickly before anyone knows that you're gone." We both knew that my pimp would not be happy to lose a good earner like me. "We'll have no fires along the way, so dress warmly."

As if in a trance, I quickly threw some of my personal belongings into a bag. Soon I felt the soft breeze in my hair as the horse galloped toward the man with the deep look, who would bring me to my sister.

Many thoughts and my whole past were running through my mind—so maybe I wasn't thinking clearly when, in the evening, I made a fire to heat some water. When my rescuer got back, he was angry.

"What's the matter with you? Thanks to that fire, anyone can see us for miles! I told you before, no fires."

Sure, he had enough patience to spend days in a pasture and slowly tame a wild horse, to twirl the lasso and catch cattle all day, or to travel for weeks alone on the trail—but he had no patience with foolish disobedience that could put both of us in danger.

Without a word, he grabbed me and set his foot on a log, then bent me over his leg, hiked up my skirt and underskirt, and with his firm hand started to show that some stupid woman was just a burden to him. It was no problem for him to keep me pinned, so I was only able to resist verbally—but I tried to make good use of that ability, swearing and cursing at him.

Unfortunately, he was not one of those who would relent because of a woman's moaning—although, true, mine were more curse words than pleas. In my anger, I wasn't in a mood to cry, but his firm hand and strong palm forced even my angry self to succumb to the situation, and so, after all, my tears started dripping into the dust of the prairie.

My bottom was turning the color of the setting sun, and with tears I started to beg and apologize to the cowboy. With the first apology, he stopped; he didn't need more. His look assured me that another stupid mistake would be rewarded even more generously.

I was furious; I felt like a small girl. Men did hurt me in my profession, but for a totally different purpose—for their own satisfaction, not to teach me a lesson. But my tears began to stop flowing as my face was illuminated by a smile of understanding. My words of apology and thanks opened another day of travel.

There were still several days of the journey waiting for us; my sister lived far away. But the incident that night kept me awake. I needed and wanted more; a new desire stirred in me, not only on my bottom but also in my lap. No man had ever impressed me this much.

The next day, when he went for water, I put a plan into action. I hid his horse, tying it behind a rock so he couldn't see it when he came back.

"Where is my horse?" His eyes bored into me.

"I … you know … I wanted to wash the dust off his head, so I loosened the reins, and he …" I lowered my eyes so he couldn't see that I was smiling.

"Foolish woman! I don't need this kind of trouble!" He put down the canteens of water, grasped my hand, and led me toward the rock. "Bend over." Hard, dry, clear.

My heart started beating with excitement and expectation. I didn't dare resist; I was the one asking for it, after all. I bent by the boulder and leaned my hands against it. He hiked up my skirt and underskirt again, and my bottom in my underpants waiting eagerly for the earned punishment. Out of the corner of my eye, I saw him cutting a twig from a nearby tree. He removed the leaves and swished it through the air several times—a heavenly sound to my ears.

I changed my opinion a bit when swish of the whip ended with a sharp blow on my bottom—but my desire for the new experience was stronger than the stinging pain that flooded my body. I enjoyed every blow and gave vent to all my pain, fear, excitement, desire, and delight. I was crying, and with every tear I was becoming stronger.

I had no idea how many stripes decorated my bottom, but like the last time, a sincere apology and request ended the stream of painful blows. Slowly I straightened, wiping away my tears, blew my nose, and quietly thanked him, looking into his lightless eyes, for the pleasurable experiences.

When the thrashing was over, he turned and went to look for the "lost" animal. The search didn't take him long. With a baffled look, he soon returned with his horse, from behind the rock. My passionate kiss was his answer. The moon shone down on us as we made love, and each of the stars was a witness to the natural intercourse between a man and a woman. There was no need for words; we both felt the excitement and desire.

We spent three more beautiful nights together before we got to the town where my sister lived. In her home, my sister and I fell into each other's arms and just cried for a long time, all the tears of our long separation.

The fact that she had sent somebody to look for me had made it clear to me that at her side, I would no longer find the domineering man who hadn't let her take care of her younger sister. Instead, her new husband was a weather-beaten cowboy with beautiful blue eyes.

The whole day and the entire evening we spent just talking—about my former fate as a prostitute, about her life as a crafty thief after her first husband's death, about her meeting with the blue-eyed man, about the end of her career as a thief, and about a cheerful wedding. The whole time, the dark eyes of my cowboy were watching me.

But in the morning, his eyes had disappeared; he was gone. Without a word of explanation or goodbye, he had taken the money for his job and vanished. I didn't shed a single tear; I was used to disappointment. I began a new chapter in my life and got involved in the events of my new town.

To such a new life undoubtedly also belongs male company and a feeling that you will be provided for somehow. In particular, I needed to pay off my pimp, so that he would not come after me. My meeting with a not-totally-poor local beau was purely business—but his purse didn't have to know that, I told myself. When I went to his house, he greeted me with a bunch of flowers and politely seated me at the table. Over a romantic dinner, the first round of our courtship could get started.

It could, if the door hadn't burst open to reveal my cowboy standing in the doorway.

"You really thought I would leave you just like that?" he demanded—a nice greeting.

Still holding the bouquet, I went to him resolutely and started beating him with the flowers. Little flowers flew all around, and I was throwing harsh words among them. He grasped both my hands, twisted them behind my back, and quieted me with a kiss. He swept me up and took me to the nearest hotel.

"You didn't say a word; you just disappeared." In the hotel room, we were talking, already calm again.

"I had to leave like that; otherwise you wouldn't let me go." I was drowning in his gaze.

"If you had told me that you would come back, I would have let you go." I was losing my newly gained composure.

"You wouldn't have believed me," he replied. "But now, I don't have to go anywhere, and neither do you."

I smiled sarcastically. "I'm a prostitute on the run; my only chance was to marry well and pay off my pimp." Again, my grip on reality came through. My courtship with the local man was completely lost, and with my mystery man, I wouldn't get much happiness—at least, not money. "One day his thugs will find me, and that will be the end." I became sad.

"No, they won't. I left to withdraw my money and pay you out. There's even something left for a small house—and then we will support ourselves."

I was in shock. It took a while for me to recover; then I threw my arms around his neck.

"Not so fast," he stopped me. "I owe you something. Seeing you with another man—that was very unpleasant."

He laid me on the bed, with a pillow under my pelvis and hiked up my skirt. There was nothing that would impede him, and so my bottom experienced the power of his belt, and I started to regret my meeting with the local man. But my cowboy wasn't harsh; that evening he had other plans, which I, with my red bottom, gladly fulfilled.

Chapter Eight

A Thrashing on a Whipping Post

In the town square, there were as many people as if it had been a fair. Just like every Sunday, the crowd was impatiently watching for the executioner and his victims. Around the whipping post, where the expected punishment was to take place, there were standing so many people who wanted to see this spectacle that the catchpole had his hands full with keeping the narrow street free, from the municipal jail to the whipping post.

Almost all the onlookers knew that there two girls had been caught stealing at the market, and today they would be punished. Many people remembered the girls shaking their nice bottoms under their skirts while the catchpole was taking them to the municipal jail, and now the onlookers were curious whether they would still shake them when the executioner hiked up their skirts at the whipping post.

In the history of the town, the council had always sentenced female thieves to a public thrashing, and the executioner would whip their naked buttocks with a broom or a withe at the whipping post. Today was no exception.

When the door of the municipal jail opened, a cart carrying the executioner and his assistants and both the girls drove out. The girls' hands were tied, and because they knew what was about to happen, they cried quietly. Today they didn't shake their bottoms; they were shivering with fear.

On the cart sat a wooden stool, on which lay several brooms and withes. When the cart reached the whipping post, the executioner's assistants took both the girls out of it and carried out the stool. The catchpole drummed and started to read the sentence. The girls went weak in the knees with horror, but the spectators rejoiced when they heard that each of them would be given twenty-five spanks.

The younger of the girls, Margaret, was to be spanked like this for the first time. Older and more beautiful Agnes had already received a thrashing from the executioner a few times before—so the executioner decided that today's thrashing would be such that she wouldn't forget it for a very long time. Although he would beat Margaret as much as the law required, he would do his best on Agnes.

He commanded his assistants to tie Margaret to the stool. Although the girl resisted, the assistants bent her easily and tied her by her waist, hands, and legs. Then they hiked up her skirt at the executioner's command. The audience exulted. Margaret's bottom was very lovely. The onlookers were looking forward to seeing how its pale skin would turn red as the executioner gave her the beating.

The executioner knew that the audience always liked it the more the longer they looked forward to it, so he gave the order to get Agnes ready too. She was supposed to be beaten extraordinarily ignominiously. The executioner's assistants ripped her clothes off and tied the hands of the shrieking, resisting, and naked Agnes high on the post. The watching men liked her firm, protruding breasts, while the women anticipated that her bottom would soon detract from her beauty, thanks to the executioner's whipping.

The executioner knew that for Agnes, waiting for her punishment would be as bad as the beating itself, because she would have to watch Margaret getting her thrashing and hear how much it hurt her.

The executioner came up to Margaret and examined her exposed bottom for a while, thinking about how he would beat her. The audience called for whipping with a broom, so he obliged them. One assistant passed it to him.

It was a fine piece of work; the executioner made a new one for every thrashing. His wife cut the birch twigs for him; they were thin, straight, and long. She had enough experience with the broom; the executioner used it at home as well. He and his wife had two teenage daughters, whom the executioner often had to thrash. He didn't tie them to any post or stool, as he did it with naughty women at the whipping post; he just bent them over his knee, hiked up their skirts, and smacked their bottoms heavily with a broom. Quite often he even bent his wife over his knee, to let her full, round behind taste the broom.

Such a thrashing was very effective; it immediately followed any misdemeanor in their home, and because the executioner knew how to handle the broom, he was also quick. The twigs of the broom landing on an exposed bottom stung sharply on the bare skin. The length of the thrashing was supposed to be proportionate to the severity of the wrongdoing, but because the executioner's daughters lay down obediently on his knee and accepted their thrashings humbly, he usually stopped after about ten blows; by then their behinds would be all red, and from their wailing it was clear that they had gotten what they deserved. But his wife resisted almost every time, and so, once he had tamed her after a short fight and had her firmly round the waist, lying powerlessly with her skirt hiked up, folded over his knee, he would give her exactly twenty-five strokes with the broom on her naked bottom.

And just that many was Margaret supposed to get today. The executioner raised his hand; the broom whizzed through the air, and when it first landed on the girl's bottom, it smacked nicely. Margaret yelled with pain, and the audience breathed out contentedly. The executioner raised his hand again and whipped the girl for the second time. He didn't hurry. He knew that the longer the thrashing lasted, the happier the audience would be, and Margaret would have more time to realize that stealing doesn't pay. She was being beaten like this for the first time—and maybe also for the last time, if the thrashing was harsh enough. And so it was a feast for the broom today.

Margaret was tied to the wooden stool so tightly that she could move only her fingers, so nothing could save her bottom, which was quickly turning red. One of the executioner's assistants counted how many times the broom had landed on Margaret's bottom: "... Twelve ... Thirteen ... Fourteen ..." She was over half of the thrashing. Margaret cried loudly; every blow hurt a lot.

"Fifteen ... Sixteen ... Seventeen ..."

The executioner continued whipping relentlessly. From time to time, he looked at the audience; they seemed satisfied—except very young Caroline, standing next to her father right under the whipping post and looking with unconcealed horror at Margaret's bottom turning red. She cried heartrendingly, and if her father hadn't held her, she would have run away from the square. She held her bottom with both hands, as if she were the one being beaten by the executioner.

She was the only one who felt sorry for the female thieves. She herself had never been beaten yet, and she was seeing a thrashing for the first time. But just when her father was about to go to the square that morning, he had found out about her latest mischief. He had become very angry, unfastened his belt, and bent his daughter over his knee. Just as he was about to hike up her skirt to give her a good thrashing, he heard the crowd rapturously welcoming the executioner as he brought his victims from the municipal jail. He realized that he would miss the spectacle at the whipping post. He commanded

Caroline to change her clothes and come with him. She would get her beating when they returned home; now she would see how other naughty girls get spanked.

It seemed to Margaret that her bottom was burning. "Eighteen … Nineteen … Twenty …" She would get five more.

The broom swished through the air, and Agnes, tied to the post, felt as though every blow to Margaret's bottom also landed on her own. She could hear Margaret groaning; she could hear the swishing of the broom and the smack as it landed on Margaret's behind; she could hear the contented rumbling of the audience, who didn't care that one thrashing would end, because they knew that they will see another—maybe even more exciting.

From time to time, Agnes looked at Margaret—at her red bottom and at the broom that was being used. She was thinking about the way the executioner would thrash her. She would rather be thrashed with the broom than with a twig—but the executioner had both with him. And when she heard the assistant counting "twenty-five," she knew that Margaret had had as much of a spanking as she was supposed to—and now it was her turn for the beating.

Margaret didn't catch the assistant's "twenty-five." She had stopped paying attention to the counting after about the twentieth blow, and she felt only the pain, which intensified with every new stroke of the broom. And when the broom landed on her bottom for the last time, she was still expecting another blow, with horror. When she realized that she had waited too long and heard the audience excitedly clapping, she realized that there were no more lashes waiting for her. She looked forward to the time when, after they had untied her, she would stroke her painful bottom, all red from the broom. It was just then that she realized that she still had her skirt hiked up and all the people could see her bare bottom, and she started to feel embarrassed. She couldn't wait to be free!

… Except that the executioner didn't intend to untie Margaret—not before he gave Agnes her beating. Even though Margaret's thrashing had been very painful, the pain would soon cease and the red bottom would be hidden under a skirt. Therefore, he left her tied to the stool even when the thrashing was over, so the girls among the onlookers could have an eyeful of her bottom and realize that it was much better to have their own behinds hidden under their skirts, rather than exposed at the whipping post, at the mercy of his broom. Also, he wanted Margaret to see Agnes's thrashing.

At the executioner's command, his assistants tied Agnes to the post with a rope around her waist, so she wouldn't thrash about too much during the beating. This time, the executioner selected a hazel withe. He liked to whip the nicely stuck-out bottoms of bent-over girls with a broom; they were firm, and every lash with the broom was nicely felt. However, when the punished woman was standing upright, her buttocks were softer, and he preferred to whip them with a withe.

He prepared the withes alone; his wife had no experience with them, because she got her spankings bent over his knee; her bottom was nicely stuck out, so she always got her beatings with the broom.

The hazel withe was straight, about as thick as a finger, and rather pliable. When the executioner swished it through the air several times, all the people knew that it would hurt Agnes very, very much. But she was supposed to get a thrashing, and the thrashing must hurt. Agnes had already had several spankings at the whipping post, so this time it was necessary to beat her really properly.

The executioner moved toward Agnes and patted her on the behind. Then he raised his hand high and swished down on it with the withe. The assistant's "One …" couldn't be heard at all, because of Agnes's shriek. On her bottom, a red weal appeared, and her body convulsed in pain.

This time, the thrashing was played out differently. Agnes quickly received ten sound blows with the withe, one after the other, and only when her bottom was striped all over did the executioner start to strike her more slowly. Agnes cried loudly, tears rolling down her cheeks, and after every well-aimed blow, she squealed with pain.

The assistant had to count more loudly: "Twelve … Thirteen … Fourteen …" so that Agnes would know how many she still had to get.

Tied to the stool and still with her skirt hiked up, Margaret watched with horror as Agnes got her spanking. Her bottom was still very painful, and she also felt very, very embarrassed. Although she knew that everyone was watching Agnes, she wanted to have her bottom hidden under her skirt. Her thrashing was nothing compared to how the executioner thrashed Agnes. Even though she couldn't stroke her bottom yet, she knew that she wouldn't have weals like Agnes's on her bottom.

What was more, Agnes was totally naked, and everyone could see how her breasts bobbed up and down as she writhed in pain by the post. Now, for sure, she wouldn't be saying that the thrashing at the whipping post doesn't really hurt and that she would let the executioner whip her bottom again, with no problem. *Never again!* Margaret resolved. Her beating still hurt very, very much—such a thrashing as Agnes's, she wouldn't want to get for anything in the world.

The executioner was now whipping Agnes very slowly, so it seemed to her that she was being beaten for ages, and surely her suffering must end soon. But the executioner's assistant had counted just nineteen so far. Six more, Agnes realized in horror as she screamed with pain. "Just five more" was heard compassionately, from the crowd.

The executioner gave Agnes hell during the five remaining blows. He saw that her bottom was already full of weals and that the hazel withe could tear the skin on her behind; he didn't want to mutilate her—but neither could he end her punishment yet; a thrashing is a thrashing. So he put away the withe and took a broom.

The broom whizzed through the air and swished Agnes over her bottom. What pain! The next blows followed in quick succession. Agnes flattened herself against the post and gasped for breath in desperation. The assistant's "Twenty-five!" was the nicest word she had ever heard.

The audience liked the ending of such an exciting spectacle, so they were leaving with satisfaction. Only a few of them lingered to watch the executioner's assistants untying Agnes and Margaret. Right away, Margaret started stroking her aching bottom. As the assistants took her and Agnes—holding her ripped dress in still-tremulous hands—back to the municipal jail, she didn't care at all that her skirt was still hiked up and her bottom was covered only with her two hands, stroking it intensely.

There was one more thrashing still waiting that day for one naughty girl. Caroline's father hurried home from the square with his crying daughter. Already, on the way, he had unfastened his belt, as if he couldn't wait to bend Caroline over his knee, hike her skirt up, and then—just as the executioner had done to Margaret and Agnes at the whipping post—give her a proper thrashing.

Chapter Nine

Bodyguard II

He undid the top button of his white shirt, poured a martini, and comfortably fell into the armchair. He'd had a strenuous day and was looking forward to a quiet evening alone. But before he even managed to take a drink, the cell phone was ringing—new, nice, modern … You know …

An unknown number.

He answered the phone. "Yes?"

"Jeremy, it's me. I … I have a problem," responded his love sadly.

"You're in the mountains with your friends; how can you have a problem—except painful legs from skiing?" He tried to sound relaxed, but his senses were beginning to heat. Why was she calling from an unknown number?

"I'm in prison," she whispered.

"*What?*" He didn't sound relaxed any more.

"Please don't panic; I'm okay. I just need you to bail me out and pick me up," she said, right to the point. Quickly, she described the situation and gave him an address.

Unfortunately, even the quick description was enough to prompt him to say, "Before I get there, you'll have time to think about how much you deserve to have your bum warmed." He hung up.

Lily hated winter. Bundled up in warm clothes up to her eyes and with a runny nose, she set out in the car toward the pension where she was supposed to meet her friend. But no luck. When she got there, her friend called to tell her that she couldn't come because she had a fever and a headache. Well, she had let her know quite soon … But still furious, Lily checked into the hotel and went to the ski slope alone; today, she would not go back home.

Nevertheless, she started with bombardino, and soon she was in a better mood. A group of young men on snowboards didn't leave her cold, so she followed them down the slope back to the funicular. But somehow she started going too fast, of course, and she wasn't able to brake in front of one guy, who was coming to the edge of the slope to have a rest.

"What are you doing, you nitwit?" She reacted in her old style as they were both rolling in the snow. Jeremy had been a good influence on her, and under his firm but amiable hand, Lily was slowly becoming a polite girl—but now he wasn't there ...

"What are *you* doing?" the man shouted back. "You're skiing like a crazy person! What if I'd been a child? Do you even know what could have happened? Ouch! I bruised my arm because of you! I ..."

"You're whining like a baby, but you're not a child," she shot back. "You're alive; so what? Adios!" And she left, doing curves.

The man just lay in the snow in disbelief, gazing after the cheeky girl.

She had been looking forward to getting back to her room after spending the whole afternoon on the slopes. She took a shower and cheerfully went down to dinner. What a mutual surprise it was when a familiar man with a bandaged arm turned out to be her waiter in the pension dining room.

"Well, see? You can even work!" She smiled maliciously and, sipping her soup, buried her nose in the book that she had brought along.

The waiter could only leave quietly, looking stunned. He muttered under his breath, "That girl, I'd really love to have her at home ..."

His arm started to itch. When she ordered him to bring a new portion of soup because there was one burnt carrot in hers, when she made him change the tablecloth because she'd spilled her third glass of wine on it, and when she had been reading the book for a long time without any awareness of her surroundings, he already had a clear idea of his plan ...

He put it into action when she ordered her fourth glass of wine. The other customers were starting to leave for their rooms, and the staff were also slowly sneaking away. Today, he was supposed to close the restaurant.

"I'm sorry, but your bill has already exceeded the house credit limit, so I have to ask you to pay a deposit," he lied smoothly and professionally.

"All right, I'll pay, but then you will refill my glass with Lambrusco, okay?" she answered lightly, with a jolly smile, and reached down for her purse.

The waiter tried very hard to suppress his smile when she didn't find her purse on the arm of her chair. Her smile faded from her face.

"I've been robbed! What kind of place is this?! Call the police immediately, do you hear me?" She was going wild.

"Of course I will," he replied. "But it's going to be to report you as a non-paying guest." He went to the phone and called the police, paying no attention to Lily's fury.

Soon, the police came and asked to search her room to see if she had forgotten the purse there. Lily knew for certain that she'd had it with her, so she was very surprised when they found her purse by the wardrobe in her room. Her surprise only grew, because soon her soft wrists were decorated with a pair of nontraditional bracelets. Shortly she found herself sitting in a cell in the police station—arrested for attempted fraud and intentional property damage

The waiter's plan was clear—he would teach the girl a lesson! Inconspicuously, he had taken the purse. Thanks to his spare keys, he could hide it back in her room. One of his good friends was the police officer on duty, so there was no trouble arranging that scene of her arrest.

He wanted to leave her to stew for a few hours, then come to her and suggest withdrawing the false charges in exchange for the satisfaction of beating her impertinent little butt. But there was a hitch in his plan: there was another policeman on duty, who had been out until just before she was brought to the station. He didn't know about the plan and had allowed the weepy girl to make a phone call ...

Jeremy arrived as soon as possible and headed for the police station right away. A young man was waiting at the entrance.

"Hello," the waiter greeted him. "You are probably Jeremy, whom Lily called."

"Yes, I am. What happened? Is she okay?" he asked impatiently.

"Yes, she is. I just ... I would like to tell you my side of the story. Before you take a swing at me, please let me finish." The waiter started to tell about the meeting on the slopes, her behavior during dinner, and his plan for the naughty girl.

"I thought I would give her a good beating, and so it would end for everyone. She would deserve it," he concluded, expecting Jeremy to jump on him.

"I agree," answered Jeremy—amused at the surprised expression on the waiter's face.

"I've just confessed to you that I was planning to give your girlfriend a good beating, and you agree with that?" the man asked, incredulously.

"According to what you've told me, that's unfortunately typical of Lily. She took advantage of not being with me and fell back into her old habits. I think you should finish your plan. But before that, I want to talk to her."

"Of course! Follow me," the waiter answered, still shocked that his plan would be completed after all.

"Jeremy!" Lily threw her arms around his neck. "I'm so happy to see you!" She hugged him before starting to grumble at the waiter, who had followed him.

"That's him; he set me up! It's his fault! He …" She trailed off, realizing which way the wind was blowing.

"You knocked him down on the slope and didn't care if he was all right?" Jeremy's voice was cold.

"Well, I …"

"Did you behave like a spoiled girl during dinner?"

"Maybe a little … but …"

"He did set you up, and then intended to suggest a deal: withdrawing the fictional charge in exchange for a well-deserved spanking," Jeremy informed her.

"What?! That bastard …"

Jeremy cut her off. "I agreed. He can thrash you as much as he sees fit, with a hand, over your panties."

He motioned to the man standing behind him. The waiter smiled slightly, got ready on the bench, and held out his hand toward the aghast Lily.

"You can't mean that, Jeremy," she pleaded. Both men's eyes were fixed on her.

"I absolutely do. If I think that you are getting more than I would give you, of course I will stop the thrashing. Don't worry; it'll be just like a spanking from me, darling," he answered sarcastically.

Lily took a deep breath to buy some time to think—although there was nothing to think about. If Jeremy hadn't been there, the waiter would have completed his plan, and she would have accepted the offer. This way, she would be beaten with her boyfriend's blessing.

At least he would stop the beating if it was too strong. He would know about the whole issue, and she would not have to face the dilemma of whether to tell him later at home about this or not ...

Okay, they won.

She took her pants off and lay down on the waiter's lap. Both men looked with a smile at her lovely bottom and enjoyed the smacking blows landing on it. Lily endured bravely, only hissing sometimes because of the pain.

After thirty blows, the man stopped of his own accord and helped Lily to stand up.

"Thank you, Jeremy, for the opportunity to beat your girlfriend's bottom," he said. "Now it's up to you." Both men smiled.

The waiter said goodbye, with a bow. "Have a nice evening; I'll see you at breakfast ..."

And Jeremy left for the pension with Lily.

"Don't pout like that; you have a face like thunder," Jeremy scolded her as they drove. "You did deserve it; you would have gotten a beating anyway. And there is one more waiting for you from me, remember. I'm getting you out of trouble again, instead of relaxing with a martini and enjoying a peaceful evening." Jeremy spoke with disappointment.

She didn't say a word; just got out of the car in front of the hotel and slammed the door shut.

Damn, Lily said to herself as she went into the hotel. *I love romantic thrashing as a foreplay, but I hate the deserved ones. Jeremy is really disappointed, and it's no use trying to argue about the punishment. It's me, again, the only one I can be angry with. If I had watched my mouth, it wouldn't have happened. Every blow hurts my bottom but especially my ego. I didn't want to lose it; one part of me still wanted to be the impudent and defiant conceited girl who always gets her way—but the rest of me wanted to be a woman that no one leaves. But I didn't manage it; I disappointed him ...* She felt like crying with anger.

She went into her room, shut herself in the bathroom and started to run a bath.

Jeremy came to her quietly.

"Undress and lean over the bath." He was unfastening his belt.

"I know, I screwed up; I'm sorry. I could have refrained from my conceited behavior." She started taking off her clothes. It was no use trying to discuss anything.

"That's true. So, hopefully, next time," he threatened lightly.

"There will be no next time. I hate the mountains." Lily smiled sadly and bent over the bath, where the water was rising—her legs nicely stretched and hands propped on the far edge of the bath, by the wall.

"Next time I'll go to the beach and be insolent with a lifeguard who pulls me out of the water," Lily teased, to lighten the atmosphere. But the first blow landed, and Lily suffered her second punishment.

"First, on a ski slope, you pay attention to what is happening in front of you, and you ski only quickly enough that you can stop in good time," Jeremy instructed her, sternly. He gave her enough time to feel every blow as he spoke, ignoring her provocation as a pitiable attempt to joke.

"Ouch. I hate skiing," Lily hissed.

Smack. "Second, if you, *by chance*, knock someone down, it should interest you whether the person is all right."

"Ouch! I should have hit him with the ski pole too," Lily fumed with rage as each new wave of pain hit her.

Smack. "Third, the staff of the hotel are not slaves."

"Ouch! It hurts! I wanted high-quality services for these exorbitant prices," she tried to defend herself.

Smack. "But excellent service would be possible even without pushing the staff around. That is four," he warned her.

Smack. "Fifth, you were drunk, alone, and you know very well that I don't like that." Three quick blows landed.

"*Ouch!* I know; I was furious at Elly that she didn't come, so I wanted to put myself in a better mood. But it was good, first-quality! I wouldn't drink just any junk," she tried to explain.

The next three quick strikes proved clearly that Jeremy really wasn't happy when she drank alcohol on her own.

"When drinking, at least do it in the company of acquaintances, because safety is the most important thing. Right?"

"Okay, fine—ouch! It was a mistake, I admit it. I'll only drink among people I know." She was fighting the pain.

Smack. "Sixth: watch your things," he continued his sermon.

"Yes, I know. That's enough; it hurts!"

Smack. "Seven. A beating usually does hurt. Say stupid information and you will get a stupid reaction."

"Jeremy!" she begged desperately.

Smack. "Eight. A man has only so much patience, so don't play with it much."

"Jeremy, I'm sorry, I'm sorry!" He really angry at her—or, rather, disappointed—and Lily truly was sorry.

Smack. "Ninth: I never, ever want to have to get you out of prison again, not even just for a joke."

"I know." She was crying quietly.

Chapter Ten

On a Business Trip with Lenka

I was on a business trip in Bratislava with my co-worker Lenka. We were dealing with a client at the edge of the city. The meeting ended, and the trip home stretched ahead of us. I was driving, and Lenka had a map of Bratislava and navigated. I warned Lenka that she had to pay attention, that it wouldn't be so easy to find the right road.

My always-confident co-worker answered that the way was totally clear, and we surely wouldn't get lost.

I offered Lenka a bet: "We will wager whether we will get lost or not. If I win and we lose our way, you will get twenty-five on your backside, as a punishment for being overconfident. If you win, you can make up any punishment for me."

Lenka answered me: "I'm sure we won't get lost, so I accept the bet. As your punishment, you will also get a thrashing."

We had to agree on the performance of the punishment so there wouldn't be any doubts later. As a place for execution of the punishment, there was only one possibility: some lonesome parking lot along the way from Bratislava.

"The one who loses the bet will have to bend over the front fender of the car," I suggested, "where we will lay a blanket that I have in back. Then, the beaten one will bare her backside and get twenty-five on the naked bottom. As the tool for the thrashing, I suggest a hazel twig. We can look for it when we stop."

Lenka answered, "You are wearing a narrow leather pants belt. That is very usable for thrashing, and we won't have to search for the hazel twig."

We also came to an agreement that to get lost meant to pass the same place in Bratislava twice.

And so we drove along, following the map of Bratislava. For a long time it seemed that Lenka would win. I was already starting to regret that we have made our bet. But then we arrived to a crossroads where a choice of the next road depended on chance—and chance was on my side. Suddenly, we were going toward the Kamzik TV tower.

Lenka tried hard to find some turn-off, so we could come back to the right direction. But her efforts were useless. Soon we were at the parking lot under Kamzik, and the only possibility was to turn and go back.

And so I won the bet. On the outskirts of Bratislava, I started to look for some suitable place where I could collect my win. It took us several dozen kilometers before we found an appropriate place that would be secure enough. Finally we managed it—although Lenka wasn't trying very hard to look for it.

I parked the car, and we got out. Lenka was wearing a red suit with a tight miniskirt. I took the blanket out of the trunk and gave it to Lenka so she could put it over the front fender of the car in a way that would be comfortable for her. I recommended that she take her jacket off, and I put it back in the car. I commanded her to bend over the front fender. I hiked her red miniskirt up to her waist.

From the red binding of the tight skirt, her bottom peeped out, covered in a pair of cheap white panties. But that was not enough. The conditions of the bet were clear. I took Lenka's panties by their edges and slowly pulled them down over her thighs to her knees. Now Lenka's bottom was totally without any protection, and the rounded cheeks were ready for a thrashing.

I slid the narrow leather belt from around my waist, folded it in the middle, and grasped it firmly.

I commanded Lenka to count the blows and warned her that if she counted wrong, she would get extra blows. After that, the thrashing began.

The first blow landed and left a thin red stripe over both her buttocks. Other blows landed rhythmically on her naked bottom, which was slowly turning red. After every blow, her bottom shivered subtly. Lenka was counting bravely and without mistakes. When we came to number twenty-five, her bottom was completely red.

I allowed Lenka to pull on her panties and skirt. We put the blanket into the trunk, got back in the car—Lenka with some difficulty—and left the parking lot. Lenka told me that this was not going to be the last bet that we made, and that next time, she would definitely win. Then she would return the punishment to me, with interest.

Chapter Eleven

Ill-Mannered Blanche

Once upon a time, at the edge of a village, there was a small cabin, where an old fisherman lived with his only daughter, Blanche. She was a peach of a girl, with long hair and a youthful figure—only her little tongue was as sharp as a razor, and her little hands were lazy.

Every young man in the village knew how Blanche could sting with her sharp tongue, and no one wanted to pursue such a cheeky hoyden. But Jackob, the blacksmith's son, who had inherited the workroom and house from his parents, was no weakling. A well-built young man, he had taken the bull by the horns after the deaths of his parents. Most of the naive girls from the village fawned on him—but what he needed was a woman. Therefore, he decided to ask the fisherman for his daughter's hand in marriage.

One word led to another, and the date of the wedding was set for the next month. The fisherman was glad that his daughter would be provided for—and that, after all, a man who liked his little hoyden had appeared. When Blanche was ten years old, her mother had died, and her father, in memory of his beloved wife, had indulged his daughter with love and allowed her to do everything she wanted. He didn't pressure her to do anything and didn't stand on any rule. But as you sow, so shall you reap, and his little daughter had grown into a spoiled, lazy, and willful young woman.

Jackob wasn't stupid; he knew that he would have to subdue his fiancée or the marriage wouldn't be possible. Actually. he thought, with a sly smile, he was looking forward to raising his minx …

When they told Blanche about the planned wedding, she started to rage like a virago. She called her father and future husband many nasty names.

Jackob just stood calmly, letting her spit tacks. When she was ready for another round of swearing and cursing, he placidly said, "Blanche, your father and I mean well to you. It is best to sleep on decisions like this. Go to sleep, and we will see each other tomorrow."

In the morning, Jackob came to the fisherman's home in a good mood; he knew that it was going to be an amusing day—and he wasn't wrong. When he entered the little cabin, the father was just cleaning up after breakfast, and Blanche was frowning right and left. The old fisherman smiled at Jackob, took his fishing rod, and went to the river.

"Good morning, Blanche, I'm glad to see you today," Jackob greeted her. "I'm happy that your father obliged me with the proposal I made. I would also like to ask you again." He knelt in front of her and from behind his back, he produced a bouquet of meadow flowers. "Blanche, will you marry me? Will you accept my protection and devotion, and will you be a good wife to me?"

She furiously snatched the flowers from his hand, threw them on the floor, and started to trample them.

Jackob remained calm. He simply said, "If you didn't like those flowers, I have some others for you," and took some hidden sprigs of birch from under his shirt.

He set the birch twigs on the table, locked the door of the cabin, and turned to Blanche. She stood, staring uncomprehendingly. When he started to crop the leaves and twist a cane, she realized what was going on. She started to yell at him that he couldn't mean this seriously and that she was not going to tolerate this.

"I only wanted to make a proposal to you in a nice way, but as you wish," he said sternly. He took her by the hand, rested his leg on the bench, and put the insolent girl over his knee. He hiked up her skirt and underskirt and started to birch her lovely butt, which for now was still hidden by her underclothes. He didn't want to pull her down naked. But to punish her—that, definitely, yes!

"You may not do this—ouch!" she screamed.

One, he thought.

"You rogue—ouch …"

Two …

"… how dare you?"

Three …

"Oww! Stop this immediately! It hurts! Aah!"

Four …

"You shit—*owwch!*"

Five …

"Stop, this instant!" She began to sob.

Six …

"Owwch! No more!"

Seven ... He was not distracted by her increasing tears. *Eight* ...
"Oww, please, enough!
Nine ...
"Owwch, it hurts so much ..."
Ten ...
"Enough of this, please ... Owww!"
Eleven ...
He could see through the fine white fabric of her undergarment that her butt was already nicely red, and her tears were falling to the ground. But Jackob had no intention of stopping just like that. If his fiancée was supposed to learn from her punishment, then, he had to be fair and consistent. More and more blows showered the protruding backside.

Blanche struggled vainly to get out of his tight hold. She cried, begged, and groaned, but it was no use. After the twentieth blow, she was already reduced to merely crying and yelling; she would have done anything just to stop the beating. Only after the thirtieth blow did he release her and let her lie, weeping, by the bench.

"You got just what you deserved, Blanche. I hope that tomorrow you will greet me more politely," he said calmly. And with that, he went away.

Blanche ran to her room and cried. How could something like this be possible? How did that scoundrel dare lay his hands on her? She would never marry him! She would never let any man bind her and take away her freedom!

In the morning, she left without a word; not even saying goodbye to her father, she sulkily swept out. Her father was worried about her, and in the afternoon, he went to ask the blacksmith whether Blanche was with him, because he couldn't find her anywhere.

Jackob thought of one place she might be, because sometimes he watched her and knew that she liked to go to a particular clearing in the forest. He calmed the fisherman's fears and set out for the clearing.

Blanche was indeed at her favorite clearing. When Jackob arrived, she was quite capably fencing with the air, using a stick for a sword. It didn't take a genius to realize who she was fighting with ...

"Good afternoon, Blanche," Jackob said calmly.

If she could have glared lightning from her eyes, he would have been reduced to a little pile of cinders. "What are you doing here, you rascal?" she barked at him. "I will never marry you! Get out of here!"

"I'm glad to see you too, my bride-to-be," he said, as calmly as ever.

That made her mad. She ran up to him and reached back to slap him across the face. But her grasped her hand and twisted her arm behind her back. He put her over his knee next to a tree stump, hiked up her skirt and underskirt, and started spanking her, bare-handed. He had more than enough energy and didn't spare impudent Blanche.

Soon, her screaming could be heard throughout the woods. First, only curse words but later, with sobs, also begging for compassion. But he had no pity for her now; as her almost-husband, he deserved a bit of esteem and nice behavior, respect, and devotion from his future wife. All he tranquilly told her while giving more smacks to the nicely red and painful behind of the tearful girl.

He finally stopped when his hand hurt—and when his minx promised him that she would change for the better. He released her and looked at her strictly.

"This will be the last time your father will be concerned about where his daughter might be; is that clear? He takes care of you, feeds you, and doesn't deserve to worry about you all day long. And I'm warning you: think about how you will greet me tomorrow."

Then he left the clearing.

Blanche soon returned home. She didn't want to risk that he might come to check her and find that she was not at home. Her tender behind couldn't have handled that.

At home, she shut herself into her room and cried all night. She knew that there was no other choice. The wedding was arranged, the dowry contract was signed, and she was going to become Jackob's wife, whether she liked it or not. And she also knew that she really did not want another beating the next day …

"Good evening, Jackob," Blanche forced herself to speak politely. "Would you like to have supper with us?"

He smiled; he knew how it must anger her to have to behave this nicely to him, but if she didn't want to get a spanking, she had no other choice.

"Good evening, Blanche. I would gladly join you; thank you. I've brought you fresh raspberries from my garden."

With a pretended smile, she took the dish. The whole evening continued this way, and Jackob had an enormously fun time watching his future wife try to behave amiably.

Over the following days, they started to meet more. They went for walks in the forest, where they talked more and slowly got to know each other better. Sometimes, when Blanche was cheeky, it was enough for Jackob to spank her and, with a hiss, she would try again to watch her mouth. He repaid her for her attempts to behave decently with small presents and kind words.

At the end of the first week, when Jackob was on his way to visit her one morning, he could hear her from afar, yelling at her father, blustering like a little girl and swearing. He entered the house and looked questioningly at the fisherman.

"It is going to be nice weather for the next two days," the old fisherman told Jackob. "I wanted her to do the washing, but she …"

Blanche sneaked a furious look at Jackob and walked past him, as if he were nothing but a waste of time, out of the house. The men exchanged clear glances. The father took a net and left too. Jackob ran to catch up with to Blanche, took her by the hand, and dragged her back into the house.

"You will not behave like this," he told her. "Your father is right; the weather will get worse, and then you will not be able to do the laundry." He drew her into the house.

"Let me go!" she ordered him. "Leave me alone; it's none of your business."

"Yes, actually, it is," he replied. "In two weeks, you are going to be doing *our* laundry."

He took her into the house. "Take off your underskirt and you're your underclothes!"

She wanted to fight him, but his cold gaze nailed her in place. She knew that she had no choice, and it was clear to her that any backtalk would make the situation even worse. Her eyes were bathed in tears. She gave him an appealing look, but soon cast down her eyes and resignedly did what he commanded her.

"Prepare the things for washing and we can start," he ordered. But first he lifted up the back of her skirt and pinned it so that her lovely butt peeped out at the world.

With fear in her eyes, she did what he wanted, and soon, in the yard, she had started her washday.

"So you won't even help me with the water?" she tried, sharply. The answer was a few smacks with a wooden spoon to her bottom and the strict remark that with this behavior, she didn't deserve any help.

Blanche then tried to do her best. Jackob sat nearby in a chair, and any time he thought that she was working sloppily, he encouraged her with the wooden spoon. Soon, the tunics and pants were soaked with her tears, and her butt shone red into the distance.

"Jackob, please, don't beat me any more," she sobbed by the washtub. "I will finish the work, honestly, I will wash everything. Please!".

"I will gladly make sure that you fulfill your promise," he answered composedly.

As she washed and rinsed everything, she wept like a little girl. In desperation, she sank to her knees by the washtub, with tears rolling down her cheeks. She turned toward Jackob and quietly said, "Please, I can't take any more; I don't have the strength. Jackob, please help me with the wringing. I will not be able to manage it."

She couldn't stand his look very long; she sank her head into hands and, again, burst into tears.

"All right, I will help you, but promise me that tomorrow night, when I come again, all the clothes will be pressed." He couldn't watch her despair any longer. She had already suffered a lot. He helped her with the laundry, and, finally, he could even see a thankful smile. Yes, that one was real.

Blanche did as she'd promised, and the next day they spent a calm evening in the town together—only she didn't feel like going to local pub; rather, she preferred to stay standing ...

The day of the wedding was slowly getting closer; the final preparations were in full swing, and to get away from them, the future newlyweds went to the forest for a walk.

"What pretty blueberries! Why don't you pick them and bake a sweet cake, Blanche?" said Jackob with a smile.

What a surprise it was when she barked out at him that she was not some berry-picker and he should pick them by himself—and as for the cake, he could buy it.

She had barely finished the sentence when Jackob was already unbuckling his belt. Speedily, he put her over his knee—and her bottom experienced the leather belt for the first time. With the first slap, she startled the animals all around with her screaming. She was kicking her legs, crying, and begging, but it was no use; Jackob was unyielding. The more blows landed on her lovely behind, the more his disappointment over her behavior left Jackob. But he didn't weaken;

more and more "black welts" colored the protruding buttocks of his bride-to-be.

After the twenty-fifth slap, he stopped and helped weeping Blanche to get to her feet. He took her by her chin and made her look into his eyes.

"I thought that we were becoming close and getting to know each other. Your behavior seemed much better. But it appears that I was wrong." He spoke in a hushed and disappointed tone. "I really don't know—with a woman who bursts out like this when a man wants any little thing from her, who is impudent over the least trifle and can't do anything for her husband just for love—whether I will be able to share the rest of my life with such a woman and give her my heart."

Then he walked away from her and left the forest.

She stood there, stunned, tears trickling down her face even more, and collapsed to the ground. *Not this*, she silently begged. With her pride she had driven away a man who annoyed and provoked her, a man whom she hated and loved. A man, she realized, such as she had always wanted, with a firm hand and a good heart.

When she had wept all her tears of pain and regret, she pulled herself together and started to think. After a few hours, she left the forest with a clear mind—and a shawl full of blueberries.

That night at home, she made dinner for her father without a murmur. She washed the dishes, wished him goodnight and went to bed. At dawn, she heard him going to the river, and after a little while she also got up, tidied the house, lit the oven, and baked a sweet cake with the blueberries from the day before. And since there were plenty left over, she baked another small cake for her father; he would be glad to have it when he came home tired.

Then she summoned her courage and went to Jackob to try to make amends. She found him in his workroom, making an ornamented handle. For a while she stood outside the smithy, but she didn't dare to enter it. Instead, she quickly rushed into the house so Jackob wouldn't spot her. She cleared the table and prepared a plate with the cake. In the garden, she gathered some flowers to and decorate the table. Only then did she go to the workroom and stand in the doorway.

Jackob noticed her when he turned to put more wood on the fire. Without a blink he continued in his work.

Slowly, she walked over to him and touched his hand. "Jackob, I ... I want to apologize."

He turned and looked sternly at her, without saying a word.

"I feel bad because of my behavior to you yesterday. I'm very sorry. Please don't be angry at me any longer; it will not happen again. Please, I'm very sorry, really. I ... made you a cake—blueberry. Will you have some? ... Please, say something ..." She cast down her eyes and waited.

He cupped her face in his hands and tenderly kissed her on the forehead. Gratefully, she looked up at him and smiled.

"I will gladly have some, my Blanche, and I'm not angry at you anymore. For the first time, you've found the courage to apologize for your fault, and I gladly accept your apology. And I'm looking forward to the cake—as long as you're not trying to poison me," he added, jokingly, and hugged her.

The next days passed in an atmosphere of peace, love—and nervousness because of the wedding. Four days before the wedding, Jackob was on his way to visit Blanche when, from afar, he could hear her shouting in argument with her father.

He couldn't believe his ears. He ran into the cabin and wonderingly gaped at the fisherman and Blanche. The old man only shrugged and left, mumbling in his sleeve something that sounded like "I told you so, daughter."

Blanche looked at Jackob's face, ran into her room, and locked the door.

He went after her. "Blanche, open the door! You're only making it worse like this! We will talk about it; what happened?"

No answer, just sobs.

"Come on, open the door." He still spoke calmly. "I will count three, and if you don't open the door, I will smash it," he warned her. He counted slowly, "One ... Two ... Th—"

The key rattled in the lock, and Blanche opened the door.

She stood before him, looking unhappy. "Jackob, tonight, there is a festival in the village. I wanted so much to go, but my father doesn't want to let me. He said I should ask you, but I was afraid to do that; I know that you don't like nights like these, and I'm sure you wouldn't let me go alone. But I would really like to go with my friends! Please, let me go; I promise I will behave myself. Please ..." She looked at him imploringly.

Jackob smiled. "I will let you go; I just hope, you won't disappoint me. Have a good time—but no capers!"

She hugged him dearly and, with thanks, smothered him with kisses.

But as it is said, trust—but also check. So Jackob changed his clothes so that Blanche wouldn't recognize him and set out for the festival as well. He sat down at an outlying table and watched his beloved, to see how she would fulfill her promise.

For most of the night, he had no reason for any objections. Blanche enjoyed the night, danced with boys from the village, and talked with her friends. But as the night wore on, one young man— half drunk—started to mess around with her. Jackob knew the boy; his name was Jack. At first he only danced with her, but gradually he grew more forward.

Initially, his advances made Blanche giggle; what kind of woman wouldn't be pleased with attentions of a man? But when he started to make lewd comments, she got fed up with him and tried to go back to the table with her friends. But Jack didn't want to let her go; he whispered in her little ear other indecent proposals. Her warning that she was engaged and so he should leave her alone didn't help; the young man stroked her face and unsteadily tried to kiss her.

Jackob was about to stand up, but when he saw that Blanche pushed her suitor roughly away and was going toward her friends' table, he calmed down. But Jack didn't want to take no for an answer; he caught up with the girl and slipped a hand under her blouse.

At the moment a loud smack rang through the hall, and the lad crumpled to the floor. Blanche was rubbing her hand, but she was still laughing at him. The other youths didn't hesitate but carried the stunned Jack out of the hall.

Jackob just smiled contentedly, drank up his beer, and went quietly home. His Blanche hadn't disappointed him; she wasn't one to fall for evening flirting.

The next morning, Jackob went to visit his fiancée. Along the way, he got an idea that he could test Blanche further yet; would she try to deceive him about the evening? Excited by the idea, he cut a stick as thick as a finger.

Blanche was stoking the oven when he walked into the cabin and kissed her neck. Surprised, she turned and, with a smile, reciprocated the kiss.

But when she glimpsed the big stick, she became petrified.

"Jackob, what is this? I … I haven't done anything!"

"You haven't done anything?" he asked, harshly—and he put on a face as furious as if she had cheated on him with the whole village. "I was given to understand something different!"

"Jackob … You mean the lad who was hanging around me at the end of the evening?" she asked timidly.

"So it's true!" he shouted at her—and the roar of his voice made the poor thing jump. "I knew I couldn't rely on you!" he continued. "Go ahead and tell me the whole truth; otherwise, you will see, you are in big trouble anyway!"

"Jackob, it was nothing; he tried to seduce me, but nothing happened. He didn't want to leave me alone, even when I told him that I'm engaged. So I shoved him aside, and when he tried to unbutton my blouse, I struck him such a blow that even today my hand hurts. Really, Jackob, nothing happened; believe me!"

She was almost crying. The whole time, she was staring into his eyes, and not even for a moment did she cast them down.

Jackob flicked the stick, and Blanche recoiled with fear. "I'm warning you," he told her, "stop lying! When you tell me the truth, maybe I will warm your bum lightly enough that you will be able to sit, at least for a while, at the wedding!"

He spoke to her very seriously, but he had to struggle not to laugh. He wanted to see whether she would admit to things that she hadn't done, just to avoid punishment.

She looked into his eyes again. "Jackob, whoever told you whatever, it's not true. I swear that nothing happened, and what I'm saying is the truth. All the spankings that you ever gave me before were deserved—but not this one." She spoke calmly and composedly; she had nothing to lose.

Jackob dropped the stick and embraced his bride. He kissed her passionately and, on the way to the bedroom, whispered, "I know, my love. I know it because I was there and saw it. Forgive me; I needed to know whether I can really trust you."

The door of the bedroom closed, and Blanche and Jackob experienced their first, for now premarital, night—well, actually, a day …

Chapter Twelve

At a Spa

The summer was drawing to an end, and the time of our second joint vacation had come. Jack left the choice up to me, and I chose a one-week stay in a spa hotel on the edge of Mariánské Lázně, which also included a package of procedures. From time to time, we both complained about our painful back or neck, and so I reasoned that massages and baths would only help us.

On Saturday we checked in, got instructions about food, a schedule of procedures, and also an offer of other activities that the hotel provided. Among them was a leaflet for a nearby spa, Kynžvart, where regular summer festivities and markets took place. Sunday's weather decided that in the afternoon, we would go there.

The band was playing, jugglers and jesters gave short performances, and there were many people everywhere. The stallholders offered mead and all kinds of candies, but also pottery, candles, jewelry, and clothes. I like to look at handicrafts, so I didn't even notice that Jack wasn't standing next to me as I went a few stalls further ahead. He found a stall full of leather: belts, but also different covers and cases, albums, key holders, and all kinds of different decorations. The owner and maker was sitting next to the stall, and his daughter was doing the selling.

Jack started talking with the maker, asking whether he takes work on contract or could customize products—and soon he was drawing sketches and possibilities that the skillful craftsman would be able to realize. The man had his mobile workshop in the caravan, and when I found Jack among the crowds of people, I only heard him telling the man that he would be back in an hour. To my interrogative look, he answered that I would see soon, but for now we would go for some tasty-smelling funfair sweets and coffee. I welcomed his proposal. The delicious scents had been making my mouth water for a while. I love candies.

We went by the last row of stalls and feasted our eyes on a skillful woman making bobbin lace and on her products. At the stall with molds, cookie cutters, peelers, and cutting boards, Jack invited me to choose a wooden spoon, because at home we didn't have a good one. I cast a black look at him and uncomprehendingly shook my head, but the salesgirl has already passed him a ceramic pitcher full of small, medium, and also quite large, round, oval, or square spoons. I took out an oval one and hissed that we didn't need one, but Jack just smiled conspiratorially. He also took me to look at jewelry; he knew that I have a weakness for beads, bijous, and just all kinds of jewels. I chose a set of a necklace, a bracelet, and earrings.

The hour was long over, so Jack withdrew toward the leather-craftsman's caravan. In a wink he came out with a package in his hand. It was getting close to noon, so it was time to get back to the hotel for lunch.

The weather held for the next few days. It was a beautiful Indian summer. The hotel staff was nice, a forest close to the hotel was an alluring spot for walks, and we were near the perfectly-kept park of Mariánské Lázně and a singing fountain. It was just beautiful.

In the afternoon, we had a snack of all kinds of sweet pastries—but I could see that Jack was thinking hard about something. It was the schedule of procedures which we received at the reception desk. For every day, it offered two or three procedures—baths, massages, or health exercises. It was clear to Jack that with a striped bottom I would not want—and it would not be decent—to lie down for a massage or to enter the swimming pool. And so he was trying to figure out how to realize his erotic spanking plans and at the same time enable me to attend the arranged rehabilitation services. He finally asked me whether I would care if he tried to re-arrange the schedule.

I have no idea what he said to the desk clerk, but in the evening, he cheerfully showed me a new schedule in which only columns from Monday to Wednesday were filled out; the Thursday and Friday procedures were scheduled for the first three days. He had even managed to pay extra money for Sunday, so we could prolong our stay for one more day. He told me enthusiastically that after the last Wednesday massage, he would be able to start giving me spankings without any interruptions.

Obviously his spirits had lifted, and he eagerly showed me the first surprise: a beautiful plaited willow switch. It was very pliable, so he had easily wound it into his suitcase so that I wouldn't find it before the trip. He was full of other ideas too, like whether I had noticed the beautiful hazel withes in the forest and many other natural tools. And so from every walk, we returned—carrying in our hands or hidden in our small backpack—all kinds of twigs and withes, which he would later clean in the room, removing leaves, tying them in different ways, and completing.

The mornings and part of the afternoons were filled with care for our mortal frames. In the evenings we had some wine, listened to the singing fountain, and even danced in a local bar.

Soon it was Wednesday afternoon. For the first time Jack showed me the product of the skillful leather craftsman, and I had to admit that the paddle was very good. On the table he in our room he laid out his other tools; to the paddle there were added the wooden spoon, a leather belt, the willow switch, brooms with different numbers of twigs and of different lengths, and a hazel withe.

His eyes were shining as he feasted his eyes on the full table—but he told me immediately that it was clear to him that twenty-five with every tool would be too much for my bottom. So he suggested that I write any number on pieces of paper with the names of the tools—any two-digit number, up to twenty-five. None should be repeated. Then, we would roll them up, throw them into a vase in the room—which contained some dried flowers—and I would draw the order and, with it, the type of tool and the number of blows. I would choose the position at my own discretion.

There was nothing to discuss. I wrote out the numbers and pulled out the first piece of paper. Jack didn't know the numbers, so he waited distrustfully to see how brave or cowardly I had been in realizing his plans.

My first draw was for his hand—and the number was twenty-four. He smiled contentedly. He had probably thought that I would just write ten, seven times over.

He sat down on a chair, I lay over his legs, and his hand landed hard on my bottom. According to our agreement, I counted—and tried not to wriggle—as an untypical twenty-four was given. Out of habit I waited for the twenty-fifth one. "Some other time," he told me.

My red bottom burned, but I drew for the second time. This time, the label called for a broom tied together from smaller thin twigs—and, with it, the number twenty-two.

I lay down on the bed, rolled up pillows under my stomach, and started counting out the strongly burning whipping. This time, he didn't leave out even my thighs, and I was silently wondering whether I hadn't overdone it with my bravery and whether perhaps I should have written lower numbers. But I would never admit that, so I set my teeth, and after a while said "Twenty-two," with a sigh of relief. Again I thanked him.

I asked Jack for a short break and something to drink. With one hand I stroked my bottom, which was only burning so far.

Another draw—the spoon, with the number twenty. Jack had a contented smile on his face as, seated on a chair, he drew me closer, and I lay down over his legs again. He adjusted the position a bit and palpated my bottom—and the spoon had a "feast."

After ten blows, he took a short pause. I could feel the first bruises swelling up. The second half was worse. After every blow, I arched my back with pain. I was happy that the twentieth blow was coming—but at the same time, I was terrified of what was still to come.

He let me breathe out, drummed a bit and scratched my violet bottom with his nails, and I slowly got up. The sight of the table, where so many tools were still waiting, augured badly for me. My initial bravery and resolution were slowly leaving me.

He gave me the vase again. I fumblingly drew the willow switch, with the number twenty-five. When I had written the numbers, the switch was the first with which the thrashing started. According to my other experiences, it was probably the most merciful tool.

I lay down on the bed over pillows, and after the first blow, I thought that I would have lowered the number if it had been possible. The switch was much more pliable and a bit longer and stronger than our other tools so far—and the main thing was that lashes were incomparably more painful.

We didn't have a headboard at the hotel, like the one he used to tie my hands to at home when I didn't obey and wanted to cover my bottom. But Jack found a solution right away. In a second, he stretched my arms upward over my head and tied them there with a scarf. The rest of the swishes with the willow continued unhindered—well, except for my groaning and moaning.

Again, halfway through, a short pause. As he ran his fingers over my bottom, I felt the first bulges and welts. Another swish and another howl from me, until finally we reached twenty-five. He untied my hands, and sighed with relief. I asked for a pause again.

In the bathroom, I wetted a towel and tried to cool my bottom a bit—but his call for me to draw again quickly ended the cooling period.

This time I passed Jack the label for the paddle and the number fourteen. I hadn't had the courage to write any higher number for this unknown tool.

I could hardly evaluate the sensation of the paddle, with so many welts and bruises. Even though every smack hurt, it was relatively bearable. Soon I said "Fourteen" and thanked Jack.

The most feared tool—a withe—I drew as the next-to-last. Considering my only—but very, very painful—prior experience with it, I had dared to write the number ten, to keep the two-digit instruction, but in brackets I wrote five, which showed my real opinion. I waited for Jack's reaction. He pretended confusion and asked whether I meant fifteen, but it was clear to him that I was trying for the lowest possible punishment.

He hesitated a moment and then offered me a choice: five medium strokes or ten small ones. More than either, I would have preferred five small strokes, but I didn't dare to say so aloud. According to the theory that this would get it over with sooner, I chose five medium ones. He moved an armchair for better access and beckoned me to get down on my knees, hold the back of the chair with my hands, and stick out my bottom nicely.

He straightened me a bit more, asked whether I was ready, and swished. An incredible pain ran through my whole body.

I screamed and pleaded for him to change to the other choice— ten light strokes. With that, I slumped into the chair. He waited till I was calmer, with the hazel withe pointed at the back of the chair, and lifted me up a bit with his hand. He straightened me several times, but the pain forced me to curl up.

Again he asked whether I was ready, and the swish came again. Another welt erupted. I burst into tears, wailing and protecting my bottom with my hands. I refused to kneel down again, despite several orders from him, so he told me to stand up. He turned the chair, and I had to bend over the rest, which was an even worse position; my bottom stuck out farther.

He tied my hands to the wooden arms of the chair; it was clear to him that I would hardly remain in that position voluntarily. To reach the handles well, I had to stand on my tiptoes. Several times he passed his hand over my bottom, looked at the welts, and instructed me to get ready for the third blow. I was shivering and just hoped that they wouldn't be so big. They were; the only difference was that the next two came in a quicker succession, because my tied hands couldn't prevent him from swishing.

Again he checked my violet-red bottom, and gave me one last swish. He untied my hands, and I started to rub my knobbly bottom, as the welts appeared, one beside the other. I asked him for a bathroom break, and with an iced wet towel, cooled my buttocks. I'd have loved not to come out, but it wasn't long before Jack shouted that he was ready.

He was standing in the middle of the room, his right leg on an ottoman. He gave me his hand and drew me closer, and bent me over his leg. He pressed his left hand firmly into my back, so my bottom was nicely stuck out and my movement minimal. The last tool would be the leather belt, for which I had chosen the number eighteen. Silently I was swearing to myself—why such a high number?—but it was too late.

The folded belt landed on my bottom for the first time. Judging by the sound, the blows were probably not very big, but carried out on a bottom that had taken such punishment already, they hurt like hell.

After ten, he lightened the pressure on my back so I could breathe out well for the last eight as we came to the finale. He indirectly proved my estimation that the blows hadn't been very strong, when he warned me that the last two would be bigger. And he didn't lie. I groaned again; not even his firm hand pressing on my back prevented from straightening up in pain.

For a long time, he ran his hand over my bottom, stroking every welt individually. He was happy that I didn't have even a small break in my skin, just bruises and welts. I was happy that the time for "giving presents" was finished.

I lay down on the bed, applying the cold towel. He watched me for a while, and suddenly he came up with the idea of taking a picture of my bottom. I didn't care much; I had my head buried in the pillow. He regretted a bit that he hadn't thought of it earlier, because he thought it would be interesting to have photo documentation after every round.

Before we had left, along with the usual drugs for fever and upset stomach, I had also added to the travel first-aid kit a tube of Heparoid ointment, which had proved to be useful in last months, making my bruises disappear faster, and a gel ice pack. I used the ice pack before dinner and then several times more that night.

On our way to dinner, the desk clerk called us over to tell us that today, they had repaired a machine for lymphatic massages, which had originally been offered among their treatments but which had had to be replaced because of the machine failure. So, the clerk offered, if I was interested, I could sign up for tomorrow. The only condition was that recipients had to wear leggings and socks in the treatment, for hygienic reasons. They were offering the massage at a 50% discount, as an apology from the hotel.

Jack immediately agreed, so the desk clerk made an appointment for me, for tomorrow at ten.

Sitting at dinner wasn't as terrible as I had feared. Jack continued thinking about our talk at the reception desk, musing that black leggings, which I wore for exercise, wouldn't show any traces. He thought that at least I should try the massage, which I had only read about so far. Conspiratorially he smiled and said that I would like it, for sure.

After dinner, he took me out for a walk, even though I didn't feel much like walking. With some movements, the after-effects of the afternoon thrashing could be perceived, but it was a nice evening, so we took sweatshirts from our room and went out. Jack carried his small backpack again, which scared me a bit that he would cut twigs and switches again. But he wanted to talk about my feelings from the afternoon's thrashing, and about the differences in tools and positions. We came to a small gazebo, and he took a bottle of champagne and two glasses out of his backpack. A walk I hadn't even wanted to go on very much became one of the nicest of our vacation.

He was enthused at my positive appraisal of the beater. We talked about various details; I evaluated my feelings about different positions in combination with the different tools. Finally, he suggested that for tomorrow, each of us should eliminate one of the seven tools that we'd used today. And if I wished, according to today's experiences, I could alter the number of strokes from each of them in such a way that the sum would remain approximately the same.

By the time we were finishing our drinks, it was totally dark, and so the little gazebo was a witness to our beautiful love-making.

Back in the room, he put the dried flowers back into the vase, and I eliminated the paper titled "hazel withe." Jack hesitated a moment but finally removed a paper reading "belt." He passed me the remaining five slips of paper, and I switched the numbers between the willow switch and the paddle, but the others I left unchanged.

Slightly drunk with wine, and under the influence of my various impressions from the whole day, I just laid the cool gel pack on my painful bottom again and fell asleep.

After breakfast, Jack left for a pearl bath. In the room, I applied another layer of the Heparoid ointment, and for one more hour just lay about in bed and browsed through yesterday's newspaper, which I had the chance to read. Before ten, I was already standing in the entrance hall, in front of a room labeled "Lymphatic Massages."

The elderly female technician explained to me briefly that, using Velcro, she would fasten me into so-called pants, which, using tubes, would inflate to compress different points on my legs, from feet to calves and thighs up to buttocks. The strength of the pressure would change regularly from weak to a mild pain and vice-versa. When she'd strapped me into the machine, she turned on some soothing music and left.

The first inflation was really pleasant, but the next felt as though it would crush my ankles and knees. The pressure rose up to my waist. At that moment, I intensely felt yesterday afternoon's blows. The inflated back of the pants was pressing hard on my buttocks, and I felt again most of the yesterday's hits and swishes. Light pressure was followed by greater, and so soft burning was followed by pain in my buttocks. I didn't know if Jack knew the principles of the lymphatic machine, but I suspected that he did, based on how he'd said that I would like it.

After an hour the machine beeped, the pants inflated for the last time, and the massage was finished. I thanked the technician and left for the room, where Jack was already reading the morning paper. He asked about the massage and how I'd liked it, and pointed at a magazine on the table that he'd bought along with the newspaper at a stand. Still in its plastic film, the title read *Marquis*.

I tore open the wrapper and started browsing through. He came and stood behind me, and we looked through it together. He found interesting a girl being whipped on her breasts. He examined the pictures in detail and tried to persuade me that we could sometimes try punishments that wouldn't land only on my backside. I rejected the idea resolutely, giving several reasons, and surprisingly, he didn't keep on the topic.

After lunch, we had a booked time at a nearby mini-golf field. The hour passed pleasantly. By a stall next to the field, we sat at a table under an umbrella and ordered coffee. At half past three, he tapped on his watch to show that was time to go, because at four, the second round would begin. I would have liked to stay there even longer, but he was relentless.

In the room he prepared five tools and contentedly checked my bottom, which was, to my astonishment, visibly less colored—and more importantly, it really didn't hurt very much. I couldn't say to what extend it was thanks to the gel and ointment.

This time, there was no drawing. He spread the pieces of paper according to the order in which we would do them. Having listened to my opinion yesterday, that I preferred contact with him—bending in different ways over his legs, not over the edge of a chair or a table—he tried to respect my wishes.

First he took the paddle in his hand and sat in a chair. I bent over his legs, and a smacking sound was heard through the room. The blows did hurt, but somehow I found them really enjoyable. I counted twenty-five and thanked him. I wanted to stand up, but the wooden spoon was already in his hand, and he had no intention of letting me stand up.

He stroked my bottom for a moment, patted it, and, with a brief warning, started to deal blows with the spoon. It hurt very much; my bottom was turning red, and I felt first bruises. He paused after ten, patted me with a hand, and began with more blows—but just four.

It confused me a bit, why he had paused after fourteen, but he gave me an explanation right away. That the next three on each buttock would be a bit harder, because after yesterday, it seemed to him that my bottom hadn't been punished enough. And really, his words proved to be true; with the next blow I bent backward and gave a moan—and on the second buttock landed a blow just as hard and painful. Only a moment's pause—and again a blow to the right, a blow to the left.

Tears were running down my face. I slipped and kicked his leg, and he adjusted me into a better position. He really enjoyed the final two blows. I couldn't even say "Thank you" because of my moaning. I rubbed my bottom and hated the spoon.

The third tool—the willow switch. He suggested that I lie down. I welcomed it; the bottom isn't stuck out also far that way. But with the first whizz, I realized that this way he also had a bigger swing. Red stripes started to appear one next to the other. For kicking my legs, I got two more over my thighs. After eleven he paused again, thumped over my whole behind, and again, as with the spoon, told me that the last three would be much harder. I had no idea why he had made this rule, because the pain of the previous eleven swishes had been intense enough. I was sobbing, and after the three remaining big lashes, I was crying twice as hard. I felt my skin swelling, and the welts were gradually coloring.

After a moment I got up and went down the hall for drinks from the fridge for both of us. When I got back, Jack was already standing with his leg up on a chair, swishing with a broom over his thighs and in the air. I bent over his knee, he straightened my position a bit, and a first swish landed. It stung terribly. With my hands I was holding the chair legs, but thanks to the pain I couldn't keep my untied legs on the floor. I was jumping around and kicking every time the broom landed. He warned me that I would get a further thrashing for my disobedient legs. And so other lashes landed from my bottom down to my knees and back. When swish number twenty-two came, I wiped away my tears, thanked him, and spent a good while rubbing my burning thighs.

The last implement was his hand. He sat down, I lay down over his legs again, and, hardly intelligibly, had to count down twenty-four. His hand was practically dancing from the right, from the left, from below, from the side—and firmly hitting all my sore spots. He didn't hurry; the end of the second round, as he said, mustn't be skimped.

When the last heavy blow landed, in a sweat and wet with tears I thanked him and went to the bathroom. There, I cooled my bottom and thighs in the shower, till I was totally cold.

Again I applied the ice gel pack for the night, and in the morning, I really felt as though the pain had subsided a bit. Jack had a procedure after breakfast, and I was happy to get back to the room, grab a book, and got back in bed. The reading put me to sleep, and I didn't even hear the click of the door. Jack woke me up with a beating, as if it were Easter. He just didn't use the switch but the paddle. I woke up when he pulled the blanket down and made my panties into a makeshift G-string.

Shaking his head in disbelief, that at ten o'clock in the morning I had been sleeping as if it were midnight, he gave twenty-five sharp spanks to my burning bottom. With his knee made it impossible to move my hand, and I couldn't disentangle my legs from the blankets, so there was nothing I could do. Each number that he counted aloud was followed by my cries of pain. He was starting to get really good with the paddle, and I had to admit that buying it had been a good idea.

For the first time during our stay, clouds appeared, and soon the rain blew up, so it wasn't the best time to go out. At the reception desk, we borrowed ping-pong paddles and keys to a small gym. He was surprised that I volleyed back quite well. Until then we had never played ping-pong with each other. I admitted that when I was young, I had played it for several years, but I was out of practice. But still, we enjoyed playing.

When we were finished, he took my hand—and he didn't have any better idea than to try the ping-pong paddle on my bottom. He bent me over the table; luckily the blows fell over my leggings, but as I was sweaty, it still hurt rather a lot. I was swearing over his opportunism, but he kissed me, telling me that he would gladly play ping-pong with me again sometime.

After lunch, we went on a necessary shopping trip to buy cookies for our parents and co-workers—but always watching the time so that the third round wouldn't start late. Back in our room, in response to my request that he cut the number of blows, since yesterday's thrashing and the thrashing from two days ago still hurt, he palpated my bottom like an expert, looked at the remainders of my welts and bruises, and promised that the blows will be smaller.

He chose the opposite order from yesterday, and so the hand began. It burnt, hurt, but there were no heavy blows at the end—and probably the blows were smaller throughout.

The broom followed in quick succession, and because of my repeated kicking and jerking, even more blows landed over my thighs this time. But because not even this seemed sufficient to him, I had to spread my legs wider and prop them from the sides against the legs of the chair so that he could lash my inner thighs. It burned terribly, and my wailing and moaning lasted up to the final blow.

Before the thrashing with the willow switch, he gave me a choice: lying down, like yesterday, or bent over his knees. I chose the second option, hoping that he wouldn't have as much backswing for the swish. The backswing might have been smaller, but I felt every swish up to the tips of my fingers; only after number fourteen was he a bit merciful.

He patted my bottom, already holding the hated spoon in his hand. Nicely slowly, the blows started landing all over my bottom; he tried not to leave out even one centimeter of my skin—and my bottom is big enough that he had plenty of space. To the accompaniment of my cries of *Ouuch*, I counted down from twenty and breathed a sigh of relief. Again, he stroked and patted my bottom—but on the table, the paddle was already waiting.

He ran the paddle over my back for a while: between buttocks and on my thighs. He asked whether I was ready, and the first spank landed. After the tenth, he took a short break, but soon the paddle was moving again, stroking my back and thighs, and another five ensued.

I tried to keep my legs on the floor, but my bottom hurt so much that I couldn't prevent a small lifting or hopping. After fifteen blows, he said that at the end, there was going to be a "small fire." I had no idea what he meant by that, but instead of an explanation, unbelievably quickly and briskly he gave me ten blows, so that my bottom really did feel as though it were on fire.

It was Friday, the next-to-last evening, and Jack suggested dropping in to a wine bar in the center of the town for a chat or to dance. On our way toward the singing fountain, we booked a table. By the fountain, we listened to beautiful music, accompanied by light effects, and then we came back to the bar. We drank our favorite champagne, listening to music from the 70s and 80s, and enjoyed a nice conversation, followed by dancing—and from time to time a trip to the bar.

Jack smacked and pinched my bottom over my light dress, and just laughed at my angry hissing. A bit drunk with wine, he started to have inappropriately courageous ideas, such as suggesting that while dancing, he would like to feel my breasts pressed against him with no bra. I pinched him lightly and reminded him that we were in a restaurant—so he should behave himself.

When the band announced the last set of songs, it was already long after midnight. We paid our tab, and I went to the restroom and removed my bra. The tiger-striped pattern of my dress didn't reveal anything, and so Jack didn't notice this change at the table. But during the final set, when I pressed myself against him, he noticed the change with delight right away, even impudently checking it with his hand, and enjoyed the last steps on the dance floor.

My legs hurt quite a lot, and I wanted to take a cab back to the hotel, but he claimed that a walk would do me good. All the way back, he pinched me all over and flicked and nibbled at my breasts, despite my scolding. He kept muttering something like "They'll get some too"—but it was very difficult for both of us to speak clearly.

I fell into bed, and in the morning I wasn't feeling my best. I heard Jack getting out of the shower and telling me to get up, that we were going for breakfast. I just shrugged it off and groaned that he should go alone. He asked me to get up one more time, but when he wasn't successful even then, he picked up his paddle.

I had no power to resist; I had a headache. The champagne, interspersed with shots from the bar, had done its job. He pulled off the blanket and didn't even have to hike up my nightdress, because I only wear ones cut above my waist anyway. A first stinging blow landed, followed by others. I have no idea how many, but finally I shuffled into the bathroom and tried to revive myself.

I wasn't doing very well. Jack had some coffee and ate his eggs and even bacon with relish; he was as happy as a lark. I was hardly able to sip my tea, and I also felt like a lark—a dead one. To my question of what was it that he had been saying yesterday night on the way back to our hotel, he answered that he didn't remember.

After breakfast, I headed straight back to bed. Surprisingly, Jack didn't hinder me. Instead, he brought out a blindfold that I had once gotten in an airplane, and which had laid for ages unused at home, until some time ago, when a scarf had impeded me from breathing a bit. I remembered it because it covered my eyes perfectly but had a shaped midpoint for the nose. When I want to sleep during the day, I need darkness for my eyes.

When I was blindfolded, Jack used a scarf to immobilize my hands above my head and started to pinch, swish, bite, and whip my breasts. There was no talk of sleep any more. Sometimes the blows hurt more; sometimes they stung a bit—but I had to admit that it was pleasant to me. The twigs of the broom and the paddle colored my breasts bright pink; they burnt a bit and hurt subtly.

At last, he untied my hands. There were two more hours til lunchtime, and he picked up that day's newspaper and let me recover and catch up on lost sleep.

After lunch, to really feel better, he suggested a walk through the woods toward the springs. He took only a fanny pack, and I took a bottle of water because I was thirsty all the time. Usually before I had changed my clothes when we would walk in the woods, but this time I stayed in the shirt that I had worn for lunch. We went hand in hand through the already well-known paths—where we had found, during that week, plenty of turn-offs with hidden benches and stumps.

Less than one hour of walking later, we left the main path, toward thicker bushes and undergrowth. He leaned me against a tree and kissed me, and tied each of my wrists with a scarf. Then, tying both the scarves together, he connected my hands behind around the tree trunk. Out of his pants pocket, he took the blindfold, put it on my face, and started undoing the buttons of my shirt. Several times, he kissed my lips and neck, and his hands skillfully undid my bra.

He knew that I only had the one with the detachable straps, because in the room, he had witnessed how I had changed the black straps to silicone ones or crossed them behind my neck, according to the type of shirt I was wearing.

He took off the bra, and my imagination, fueled by fear, started working at full throttle. I heard different noises as he broke and cut withes and twigs or weird plants, and I shivered with excitement and fear. Again he started to kiss and suck at my breasts—but noticeably more callously, giving me some slight pain. Even squeeze of my nipples with his fingers was hard, making me groan.

The scarves on my hands didn't allow any movement, so I could only scream when the first swish landed. Immediately the second and third one followed. They burned quite a bit; some of the plants must have had tiny thorns, because they prickled unpleasantly. Several times I yelled out, partly in shock, partly with pain, but he admonished me that it was not appropriate to yell in the woods—and that for yelling, bigger swishes would come so that I would remember it.

Stroking and kissing my reddening breasts was followed by more swishing, until I bent backwards. My nipples stuck out from fear and the irritation of the beating, and he squeezed them with his teeth until I groaned. His palms were stroking my burning breasts, and his fingers pressed my nipples hard. I tried to beg that it was enough, but he silenced me with kisses and told me that *he* knew when it would be enough. And again, a swish from above, then from the side, and then to the undersides of my breasts.

Now and then he would change the regular swishes, taking the withe and swishing one breast intensively. Some swishes were so strong that I couldn't keep from shouting. I got two sharp swishes as a punishment, and he started swishing my other breast.

Then I came in for two stronger swishes, but again he covered my breasts with kisses, together with kneading and rubbing. My breasts already burned and hurt, but he returned with several other twigs that he had tied together, and swished them regularly from all directions. At last he suggested that I count twenty-five finally; he probably didn't know any other number. Naively I thought that that would mean twenty-five in all, but he carefully gave the full number on both the right and the left.

With his fingers, he rubbed and pulled my nipples a while longer, so that I arched my back. He removed the blindfold from my eyes, and I unbelievingly looked down to see that my breasts were of the same red color as the checkered pattern on my shirt. Jack liked that comparison a lot. He untied my hands and put my bra into the fanny pack, so that on the way back to hotel he would have better access for checking the hotness of my breasts. And along the way, he did as he'd promised, several times.

Chapter Thirteen

Pirates

With her last gasp, she scrambled up the wooden plank that was floating nearby. The last thing she felt was the sea; the last thing she saw was the sea; the last thing she heard was roar of the sea—then just …nothing.

The first thing that she realized was that she didn't feel anything from the sea any more. The world swayed, but it was dry. The air smelt of salt but was dry. She heard the waves, but she was dry.

Slowly she opened her eyes—and even more slowly she managed to sit. She was in a ship's cabin, with a bandaged hand, a tray with food and tea, and great uncertainty about what waited behind the door. She wrapped herself in the cotton counterpane and resolutely went out. Wherever she was, she was the daughter of a well-known merchant, and that would ensure her return home.

Slowly she made her way through the passage to the stairs up to the deck and climbed them toward her destiny. She took a breath of the warm sea air and looked up at the warming sun. Then she saw it: a fluttering black banner, with crossed bones and a white skull.

She was struck dumb with horror, not even realizing that the men on deck had become quiet. Her eyes filled with tears. *Not that! Pirates …*

She was about to go back to "her" cabin when she heard a voice that sounded stern, firm—but kind: "Welcome aboard, missy."

She turned and saw him coming toward her: a tall, well-built man wearing cloth pants and a white shirt, his hair tied into a braid with a shawl, and a knife and gun clipped to his belt. The captain.

"Welcome," he said again. "My name is Marcus, and I'm the captain of this ship. We found you unconscious in the sea. Who are you, and what happened to you?" he asked politely.

What? A pirate? How dare he ask her anything?

"I'm the daughter of a wealthy and well-known merchant. I want to go immediately to Nulister Port, where I live—and I refuse to speak to riffraff like you," she let fly at him saucily and put her hands on her hips.

The crew had a hard time not bursting out laughing, but they were curious about how this scene would play out.

He smiled, and his eyes flashed. "I'm riffraff? It's you who doesn't have a penny to your name, a roof over your head, or anything to wear." With a quick motion, he ripped off the counterpane. "It's me who will not speak with such a cheeky pauper," he said with a smile—but his eyes were absolutely serious.

He really hadn't expected such a beginning; what kind of a brash and arrogant hussy was she?

She was as red as beet, standing there naked in front of all those barbarians.

"So, to clear the air, miss, I honestly don't care whether you are the daughter of a fisherman or the king of England. Now you are on my ship, and we follow my rules—and one of them is that we treat one another with esteem and respect. My life depends on work of these men, and their lives depend on mine, and that applies to you as well; is that clear? So no one is interested in your haughty twaddle—but about your pretty young body, probably everyone is. So control your impudent mouth; otherwise you will often end up here naked." He spoke firmly and covered her again with the counterpane.

He took her to the cabin.

"I want to go home." She started to cry. "Please, take me to Nulister Port; my father will pay you richly. Please," she sobbed.

"That's not possible; we are heading south with our freight. We will get to Nulister in six weeks. Until then, you are like a crew member. You will take part in the work, and you will get food, a bed, even clothing—and my word that I will take you to your parents' house. In the closet, there are some clothes. Once you're dressed, come above; I will introduce you to the crew and show you the ship." He tried to comfort her. He felt sorry for her; the young lady clearly hadn't experienced life outside her golden cage yet.

She stayed in the cabin alone. Unhappily she dressed, took some food, and fell into a sullen sleep on the bed. The captain let her rest.

Her first thought in the morning was of escape. She absolutely could not stay here with these pirates; she would get home, even without them. She slunk out of the cabin, slipped through a rear hatch, and went up on deck. The men were still having fun at her expense, so they weren't paying much attention to their surroundings in the early morning. Quickly she got to the rail and dove into the water.

"Man overboard!" someone yelled—the ship began to boil with activity. Ropes and a ladder were cast, and someone dove from the ship and quickly swam toward her.

"*You?*" said the pirate, with surprise, when he caught her. He grabbed her and drew her back to the ship on the rope.

It wasn't long before she was standing in front of the captain, Marcus, staring fixedly at the floor.

"With your foolish attempt to escape, you've endangered my men who had to rescue you," he said sternly. "Your behavior is more than unseemly. To understand that at sea we don't excuse mistakes, you will receive twenty-five blows." He reached out for a thin whip that a man next to him was handing to him.

The men grasped the poor girl and tied her to the mast. They pulled off her skirt, leaving her with only a thin blouse.

"No! Not that!" she cried. "You can't do this; my father …"

"Your father is not here, and you do deserve your punishment. I only hope that it will be a sufficient warning to you, not to try any further silliness," he said, strictly.

Then the first blow was given. The poor girl shrieked, and the ropes dug into her wrists. The second, third … She yelled and screamed, cried, and begged … The whip twisted around her young body. More and more blows landed on her bottom, back, and thighs. The fine fabric of her blouse was no protection from the pain. She cried, begged, and promised, but more waves of pain flooded her spoiled body. By the twenty-fifth blow, she was about to faint. Her body was covered in blood-red stripes—but there was not a drop of blood spilled; the captain didn't want to hurt her. If she only knew how he had restrained his strength …

"Take her to the cabin—and, John, you are a doctor; look at her. Thank you."

Everyone else went back about their business, but they all had the same thought in mind: how could that the girl they had saved be so impudent?

She woke up in the morning with her whole body hurting. She slowly sat up and stared at a pirate who was sitting in the cabin, his legs on the table, and cleaning his dirty fingernails with a knife.

"Morning, damsel," he greeted her. "I'm supposed to be your nanny today, so just dare to cause trouble. Oh, and you are supposed to eat the breakfast that's on the table, or I can stuff it down your throat by force—so said the high muck-a-muck." He cast a bored look at her.

The last thing she wanted now was any personal contact with this individual, so without any protest, she ate the food—and with a good appetite; after all, she hadn't eaten much yesterday.

Then her guard took her on deck, and the captain took charge of her. As he had promised, he showed her the ship and explained the basics of how it worked. With a sour face, she nodded to everything he said—and gaped in disbelief when he placed her in the charge of a man who was repairing the fishing nets. The captain said the old man's name was Ben. She was supposed to work off her stay on the ship, just like the others, and she would begin here. At least she would have a view of events on the ship, she reflected. Although if she wanted to run away, her nanny was close at hand …

She was supposed to work? Well that was a joke, wasn't it? She stood by the nets and angrily held them while the old man was mending them. As she stood there and pondered, she toyed with the strings—and after a while she released some, made a loop, ripped a battered part, and maliciously smiled. She tutted; *Me and work …*

"What are you doing, you butterfingers?" shouted the old crewman, and plucked the net out of her hands. Soon, the captain and her nanny were there; at a glance they both recognized that these were not just accidental mistakes but intentional damage.

"Ben, she is destroying your work, so you yourself will decide her punishment," said Marcus calmly.

Ben didn't hesitate; put the damsel over his knee and with a heavy hand dealt her fifteen strong blows on her butt. The little miss was yelling like a crazy woman and bawling curses at him like a real crewman. While she blustered and cried, the crew had a fun time.

"I don't have to warn you that this will not happen again, do I?" said Marcus quietly after the beating. "Fish are the main source of our living, and the quality of the nets is essential. That's why today you won't get any lunch." Roughly he took the resisting damsel below deck to the kitchen—the galley, the sailors called it.

"You will spend the rest of the day here, helping our cook, Francis —and you will not taste even a bite. Clear?"

But even here she proposed to spite him; how could they even think that she would work? Strewn potatoes, a broken bowl, unpeeled onion in the food… The cook was running out of patience by the evening; he bent her over his knee and paddled her with a wooden spoon. Her yelling soon summoned the captain, who stood in the doorway, smiling contentedly as he watched her painful beating.

"I don't know if it is a good idea to continue in your willful acts," he said, in amusement. "By the time the voyage is over, you might not be able to sit. Francis, thank you for saving me the trouble."

"You're welcome, captain." The cook ended the beating and wiped away the beads of sweat on his forehead.

Through tearful eyes, the girl looked at the captain wrathfully and fled into her cabin.

"When dinner is served on deck, you will be expected," He called after her.

On deck, the whole crew were having a good time, enjoying the evening peace—and vastly amused at her attempts to sit comfortably. The captain's look said simply, *I warned you; you'd better start behaving yourself.*

The next day she behaved quite tolerably. She didn't say a single word, and—though she made an unpleasant face—did at least a bit of what she was supposed to. The captain's attempts to talk to her were useless; she ignored them all. She didn't come out of her annoyance until the evening, when she got a slap from the captain because, for the hundred time, she had acted as if she hadn't heard him speaking.

"I really don't have any special liking for beating young women, but you are asking for trouble. I'm trying to speak to you, to find out who you are, so it's in your interests to oblige me, please," he said placidly.

Resignedly, she told him about her studies of art in London, from which she had been home for holidays when the ship had foundered. She told him about her rich father and the beautiful house they lived in. Then she went to bed.

The next days passed very similarly. Marcus assigned her to individual crew members in turn, to help her get to know life on the ship. Sometimes she got a spanking when she made deliberate mistakes out of spite. But the last straw was when she drilled the barrel of drinking water, which ran out during the night.

I will teach them—morons, she told herself. *They will have to restock the water, and in the port, I will escape.* That was her plan.

In the morning, the door of her cabin flew open. A man pulled her out of her bed and dragged her up to the deck and flung her down in front of the captain. The crew was assembled around.

"Missy, this time you've gone too far," the captain told her, very sternly. "The drinking water is more valuable than gold at sea. For what you have done, each man of my crew will punish you." An affirmative muttering was the crew's response. The captain was very angry, and it took a lot of effort to retain his self-control and not beat her immediately, on the spot.

They tied her by the hands to a raised spar and ripped off her nightdress, leaving her in only her underwear in the middle of the deck. Marcus came to her with a three-headed cat.

"Every man will give just one stroke—and not over her head. I don't know yet how many turns we will take; we'll see," he told the crew drily. Looking straight into the girl's terrified eyes, he passed the cat to a man on his right.

The first blow landed, and the damsel screamed with pain, She had never experienced pain of such a beating—had never experienced anything at all like this. She arched her body under the second blow, and the cat traveled to a third man. Another blow, another cry, and more hopeless tears.

The men slowly begin to switch, and the girl experienced hell. Some gave stronger and some slightly less strong blows; some to her back, butt, thighs, and calves; some, for a change, to the fronts of her legs. They weren't barbarians; no one was aiming for her belly or chest—but also no one protected her.

Desperately, she yelled, shouted, swore, and begged, but to no avail. After each stroke of the three-tailed whip, thin red stripes appeared on her shaky body. After the thirteenth man, she got the last one from the captain.

The girl no longer had the strength to yell; she just softly asked for mercy.

"The second round," was the quiet verdict. Marcus hoped that such a harsh punishment would force her to behave better and no longer endanger the lives and health of the crew. He wanted to give her a lesson.

No-o-o, was the thought flying through her mind; *this can't be true.*

And it all began again. The men traded off; their blows may have been softer, but still the girl's aching body received them as if they were hot irons. She wriggled on the rope, groaned with pain, cried, begged, promised, pleaded for compassion. She prayed for the end of this suffering, but in her heart she knew that she deserved it; this time she really had gone too far. If a storm had blown up, they could have been in danger, and the lack of drinking water could cost them their lives. This was not London, with all its comforts; this was the sea—uncertainty, a fight for a life, a fight against the raw forces of the elements, harmony with nature, and teamwork ... Now the question *How could I have been so stupid?* was running through her head, while her young body was punished with more and more blows.

The last stroke came from the captain's hand. They all were waiting for what was going to come next.

"You know that this isn't the whole punishment for endangering all of us. The complete punishment is throwing the offender overboard. Untie her," he said, without a blink.

The prearranged performance continued.

Even in her position, she was able to perceive the horror that gobbled her up; it was the death sentence after all ... They untied her and guided her to the open rail. Two men held her up and looked expectantly at Marcus.

"Jump," he said firmly. He was a good actor.

"No, sir, please, not this! I don't want to die," she whispered supplications for pardon. "Captain, please, I will never do it again! I won't do anything of that kind any more! I will ... I ... I will try to work well here. Please ..." She no longer had any strength; she burst into hysterical tears.

"Crew, does this impudent creature deserve a second chance?" Marcus asked his men, as if nothing had happened—and he had a hard time not laughing.

A quiet muttering of disagreement slowly changed into occasional *Aye; yes; all right; we'll see; give her a chance, Captain.* They played the prearranged game. Finally, the men unanimously agreed to give the damsel a second chance.

Exhausted by her screaming and crying, dazed by the pain, and full of hopelessness and fear, she ended up back in her cabin. The crew's doctor smeared her body with a healing balm, and gave her some medicine to drink, and speedily sleep smothered her suffering.

She fought against waking up; she didn't want to come back to reality. Every part of her body tingled and hurt. For a long time, she just lay with her eyes closed, wondering what was going to happen next. She did not want to accept the defeat and keep her word. But she had to admit she was impudent and bossy—and she knew how important the power of a vow should be. She also realized how stupid her behavior had been. Slowly she organized her thoughts.

At last, she gathered her energy to stand up; she dressed and walked onto the deck. The men fell silent and gaped at her, and her eyes met those of the captain.

"Good morning, captain," she said, looking an unspoken apology into his eyes. "Good morning," she said to the men.

Marcus smiled at her, and the crew murmured a greeting and returned to work with relief.

She asked the captain to speak with her in privacy.

In the silence of his cabin, she apologized to him: "Sir, my behavior was foolish, and I'm very sorry. You saved my life, you provided me with nourishment and care—you could have left me at sea or thrown me overboard because of my behavior. You don't deserve to have been treated so arrogantly and impudently in return. Your crew is a team of good men who stand behind you, and you lead them well. I am sincerely sorry for my behavior; it will not happen again. Until you drop me at home, there will be no further problems with me, I promise."

It was the first time she had ever apologized frankly; it was the first time she knew that she was doing a good thing.

He smiled at her, but he knew that if she was supposed to take a new view of life home with her, she would have to get another lesson yet.

"I accept your apology, and I truly hope that you will try to not make problems. There is a lot of work waiting for you here." He knew that this was true not only on the ship but also on herself...

She did as she had promised, carefully watching what she was supposed to do and how to do it. Day by day she learned new things: how to mend nets, how to cook; she scoured the deck, folded sails, cleaned the ship, and cleaned the cannons. She behaved decently, amiably—sometimes she even smiled—and there was no problem with her.

The crew grew to like her, and the time they spent together was a benefit to everybody. They taught her about the secrets of the sea and the sky, and she told them about the city she lived in, about history and science. Marcus was satisfied, but he kept a stiff upper lip. Treating her as if she were a dog, he only set commands and controlled the fulfilled tasks. He was cold and hard, giving her no words of commendation or praise, only new duties. He wanted her to learn how society behaves toward its dregs; he wanted her to think about herself. So she worked even harder to prove that she did deserve her life.

After a week, she was so exhausted that she didn't know what to do. One evening at sunset as she was standing near the fore, tears began to flow down her cheeks. Marcus came to her and started scolding her for loiters when she still had work to do. Deliberately, he kicked the bucket that stood nearby on the washed floor.

She said quietly, "The whole week, I've been trying to keep my word. I work to the best of my abilities, I do your bidding, and you? Nothing, no thank-you, no *well done*—nothing; you just keep ordering me about and disparage my work. I don't know if you are still punishing me for my past transgressions. I know I did behave terribly, and I'm sorry. I just miss a bit of appreciation and respect. I … I'm just a human being. I'm at the end of my rope. That just …"

"And so the circle has closed," he interrupted, smiling. "At our first meeting, I wanted from you esteem and respect for me and for my crew, and now you are asking the same. During the past week you've proved that you also deserve it. I've been very satisfied with your work and behavior, and I hope that all of this has been a sufficient lesson to you and that the rest of the voyage will pass in a friendly mood." He smiled at her.

She turned to him and smiled. "So even this was a lesson?" She cast down her eyes.

They both were standing by the prow, savoring the balmy evening.

After a while, she spoke to him again. "I wanted to tell you something else too. I was mistaken about you—about you all. You are not a band of barbarians who revel in robbing and killing. I have heard your conversations with the helmsman about who you want to attack and rob. I recognize the names, from my father. You never once mentioned the honest traders. It's the dishonest, with cheap goods, whom even my father grumbles about—those who steal from their customers—those are the you choose for your targets. It doesn't excuse what you do, but you have more principles and honor than your victims."

Surprisingly, he was silent. He hadn't known that anyone had been listening—least of all her.

She spoke again. "I also heard you saying that the profits from your next raid are meant to be for the reconstruction of a school." And she gave him her gold bracelet. It was the first time that she had ever shared anything of her own.

With a smile, he took the bracelet. She smiled back at him, knowing that when she returned home, nothing would be as it used to be; she would not be as she used to be. The vain damsel had been carried away by the ocean. She would return back home as a new girl—and only she and the pirates would know that it wasn't London that had changed her …

Chapter Fourteen

An Advertisement

When Mark told me that he had received an offer for one-year stint in America, the information took me by surprise. A lot of moments, the thrashings and fun that we'd had together, ran through my mind. Outwardly I answered bravely that it was awesome. I was among the first people he was telling about the details of the trip, and it was clear to me that such an offer was not to be sneezed at.

A few years ago, a chance had brought us together. One Saturday evening, both of our former classes had a reunion in the same restaurant. A group of my high school classmates met in a smaller private room, and his elementary school reunion was taking place in the bigger one. When we had reminisced about everything after so many years, looked at the pictures, and exchanged current phone numbers, slowly my classmates who lived in remoter cities started to leave. Those of us who lived locally moved into the bar and invited one another for drinks.

It was great fun there; in the next room, a disco blared for over an hour. I was getting down from my bar stool when I heard someone observe, from behind me, that I hadn't finished my drink—and in front of me, a full glass appeared. I turned uncomprehendingly, and a handsome man told me that the drink was in exchange for a dance. We clinked glasses and went to the dance floor. There were already many people there: fast songs alternated with melodies from our school years. His name was Mark. We found out that each of us was attending a class reunion, but we didn't get back to the subject.

He and I spent the rest of the evening talking, and around midnight we were about to leave. We met two of my classmates—evidently tired, supporting each other as they walked—who reproached me for leaving the group in the private room. They said that I would deserve some punishment. Mark replied right away that he would undertake the task. We laughed and said goodbye. My classmates and I would see each other again in five years.

I wanted to take a cab, but Mark persuaded me that a walk would do us good, and told me that he would be glad to escort me home. We went through a lonesome forest park, remembering our school years. He told me that he had finished high school away from his hometown, and that he had lived there for several years afterward.

Then, totally out of the blue, he turned the conversation to the last sentence of my classmates' goodbye: when and where was he supposed to take care of my punishment?

Rakishly, emboldened by the alcohol, I answered, "Here, if you like; no problem." But I added that in five years, before our next class reunion, no one would remember that remark.

He didn't let me change the subject any more. He was trying to decide whether to take the belt from his jeans or break off a withe. I was surprised that he actually seemed to intend to do it—but I figured, *Why not? After all I've never had a thrashing on the way from a restaurant.*

He found a hidden bench in the bush. He sat down and bent me over his knee, and a first blow with the belt landed on my bottom. It stung, but my skirt absorbed the blows quite well. After about five blows, he started to urge me to hike the skirt up. The thought of getting my thrashing over nothing but my thin panties attracted me, and so I pulled the tight skirt up above my waist, and the belt hit my buttocks again.

Without asking me, he adjusted my panties so that other blows could land on my bare bottom. They hurt, stung, burnt. I tried not to cry out, but I couldn't hold back the shouts of *Ouch!* and groaning. He stroked my hot bottom for a while and scratched it—which was amazingly pleasant. He warned me that the last five would sting more,—and he wasn't lying. This time it was me who was stroking my painful bottom and slowly pulling down my skirt.

We went on toward my house. I was terribly confused—partly thanks to the alcohol, which was beginning to lose its effect, and partly thanks to the influence of the experience of the previous moments. We exchanged phone numbers and goodbyes.

I couldn't fall asleep, and all the next morning I wondered whether it was normal to behave like this in mature years. I had been divorced for less than a year; I wasn't looking for any serious relationship—one bad experience was enough so far. My contemplation was interrupted by the beep of a text message: Mark was asking how I felt and whether my bottom hurt much—and he told me that he would like to see me again.

We met, symbolically, by yesterday's bench. The park looked quite different in the daytime than at night.

As we talked, he told me that he had moved away from his girlfriend to his grandmother's place and that he was looking for an apartment—but because his grandmother lived at her cottage from spring to fall, he had almost half a year to solve this question.

We slowly walked through the whole park and came up to a row of older houses. He told me that this was where his grandmother's apartment was. I didn't really want to go to somebody else's apartment, but fine rain played into his hands, so that we decided to hole up at least for a while.

The conversation turned soon to the previous night. He wanted to make sure that he hadn't given me any welts or bruises. I resisted to no avail, trying to tell him that everything was okay. I felt a bit embarrassed; yesterday's alcohol wasn't protecting me any more, and the reality was worse. He drew me closer, undid the button of my pants, and with no difficulty, pulled my loose pants down. I regretted a bit that I hadn't worn jeans, as I had originally intended—the tight ones that I always have a hard time getting up or down.

He was nice, though, and something about him attracted me. In all his natural conversation on the topic of thrashings and so on, he definitely wasn't unsympathetic to me. The check of my behind turned out badly: almost no marks. He regretted that he had spared me too much. But he promised to rectify that right away. Despite my mild resistance, he bent me over his knee again, and his hand started to smack my naked left and right buttocks by turns.

Pain was followed by stinging and burning. Eventually, he interrupted the blows and tapped and stroked my bottom. He was saying quietly that at first it was good to warm up the bottom by hand or with a leather paddle and then color it a bit with, for example, a wooden spoon or a withe. He had both the tools prepared, and so, while I groaned and moaned, he colored and painted red stripes and, with his other hand, warmed up with the spoon.

This time he was satisfied with the result—and it was like that every time, almost the whole three years. He found a girlfriend, but she didn't want to even hear about these practices, much less to watch them or participate in them. And so we kept meeting peacefully until the date of his departure to America came.

Very often after he left, we exchanged emails, but the topic of thrashings did not come up in them. I had no idea whether some similar opportunity had come his way there, and I hadn't had any new experiences with anybody else so far. From time to time, a worm of temptation gnawed at me, but I didn't have the courage.

One fall Saturday, when the rain was beating in sheets against the windows, I was sitting in front of my computer. Memories led me to Mark again, and I had to confess to myself that I was missing his firm hand. I was going through websites focused on spanking; I read several new stories and clicked on some personal advertisements. By a process of elimination—considering locality, age, and also the ideas of the advertiser—there remained three to which I decided to reply.

One went unanswered, and the second man had a much harder vision than he had stated in the ad. I thanked him and said goodbye; there was so sense in keeping up the correspondence. The third one seemed confident; he described his experience and warned me that he was married—which was fine with me; I wasn't looking for a relationship this way. The emails were concrete, and their reading aroused me pleasantly.

He suggested a nonbinding meeting. Some things can be explained better face-to-face; in a written form, they can come across wrong.

At my suggestion, we met in a coffee bar at a shopping center, about halfway between our homes. He had declined to send a picture; he just gave me a phone number in case of any unexpected change.

I arrived at the shopping center early. I went through several small stores, and a few minutes before the arranged time, I went over to the coffee bar. In front of it waited was a tall, athletic man with close-cropped hair, his age apparently corresponding with that of the man from the ad. There were about five minutes left, and I faltered as to whether this nice-looking guy was really *him*. Because of the number of women passing by, he probably shared my uncertainty, because a text message, with information about the clothes that he was wearing, beeped on my phone. At that moment there was no doubt, and I went toward him.

We sat at a table in the back of the coffee bar, and I realized that I was very nervous and that communication—by which I make my living, after all—was suddenly giving me difficulty. The self-confident, almost infallible behavior, that I had already sensed from his emails, proved to be true more and more. Something attracted me powerfully to him—but at the same time also made me wary. When I came back from the restroom, he had already paid and waited for me with an offer to go to his office, where we could talk more and decide whether the proposed plans would be realized.

It took me by surprise; we had a clearly agreed on a nonbinding meeting in the coffee bar—but he didn't give me much time for thinking. I had to concede that my meeting with Mark had also been an unknown adventure at the very beginning, and so I nodded. He didn't want me to follow him in my car, because he wanted to talk about our ideas in the car, and then he would take me back.

We stopped at the edge of the town, in an industrial area, where a lot of companies had offices. From a spacious hall way, we entered a smaller office. He offered me a drink and invited me to go and look into the next room. He said that he spent plenty of time there—and his athletic figure indicated that he was not lying. It was something between a gym and a weight room, with two new fitness machines, a set of old wall bars, and a vaulting box in the corner; probably equipment from an old school gym. We went back to his office; I felt a bit embarrassed. It was mainly him who was talking, and more and more I had the feeling that my ideas and wishes, about which I had told him in the car, weren't being acknowledged.

I regretted that I hadn't driven my own car; the possibility of leaving would have been much easier. His opinions that there was nothing to lose and nothing to be afraid of, that he would find out exactly what I liked and what I didn't, commanded more fear than trust.

I had to admit that he was dominant—but I hadn't imagined a dominance like this. Mark was also dominant; he didn't even have to speak and his gestures would be clear, but never, not even for a minute, had I been scared of him. The blackest thoughts were running through my head; my imagination was operating at full capacity. I tried again to open the debate, admitted that that I was a coward and felt queasy about it—but he didn't seem to listen.

In the gym, he moved the bench away and gave me an explicit instruction to assume a position by the wall bars. The only part of my wishes that he honored was letting me keep my T-shirt and panties. I was nervous and in a cold sweat. I had no courage to turn and see what he was rattling behind my back and what he was doing with his hands. He showed me which of the wall bars I should lean on with my hands so that the forward bend would be sufficient—and, for the first time, the leather belt landed on my bottom as it stuck out.

I don't know whether the pain was compounded by fear; I had also had nice welts a couple of times from Mark, but it had never hurt this much. I cried out, let go of the wall bars, and tried to protect my buttocks with my hands. He grabbed my arms, put me back to my original place, made a G-string of my panties, and warned that I would get even more for my disobedience. I had no doubts about his words. I was only resolved not to let go of the wall bars and not to provoke him. I hoped that rest of the blows would be minor, and that maybe his words, that I would like it, would come true.

Another blow on my bare skin burnt even more, but my hands didn't move. A short pause and again a painful spank, and another and another. To keep my legs on the floor and hands on the wall bars, and hold back the tears that were welling up in my eyes, was beyond my strength. I couldn't top myself from groaning, sobbing, and letting my body jerk.

He took a pause, stroked my bottom with his hand, and tapped it lightly, and I naively hoped that he would reduce the severity of the blows and that the thrashing would take a different tone. It did—but only thanks to a change in the tool.

He pressed my back strongly with his hand so that I would really bend forward, and the paddle landed with a smack on my bottom. I didn't know which was worse. In Mark's hands, both of these tools were pleasant to me. I had also said in the car that I hated the withe and didn't even want to taste a cane. Here, both the belt and the paddle seemed brutal; the blows were much bigger than I was used to, causing a severe pain. If it was true, as he himself claimed, that he had enough experience to recognize when to ease off and when to step up, he should already—a long while ago, after the vigorous beginning—have eased off.

Another painful smack interrupted my thoughts. I felt the weals swelling up. My bottom was red, and I was shivering and moaning. The last blow with the paddle, and I could finally straighten up with relief. I had an intolerable pain in the small of my back. I mustered all my strength and courage, and asked for an end. My words probably surprised him, but he didn't let me change his planned course for the evening. Despite my resistance and a last try asking for him to finish the thrashing, he bent me over the old vaulting box, and a wooden spoon hit my bottom.

A mixture of pain and anger—at him and also at myself, that I had let him talk me into leaving with him—were followed by screams and moaning. My back didn't hurt as much any more. The front part of my body was lying on the leather lid of the vaulting box, my hands clutching convulsively at the side, because I was afraid even more of his threat that he would tie my arms if I put my hands on my bottom. Every blow increased the unbearable pain. I was crying, and my only wish was for this to end.

When he put away the spoon and again tapped my buttocks, I hoped that he was satisfied and that the end had come. But it had not. He straightened me a bit, and a cane swished through the air. I shouted, let go of the edges of the box, and, still crying and sobbing, yelled "Stop, enough!"

He waited a bit until I calmed down—and uncompromisingly commanded me to get back into the original position if I didn't want to be tied up. Escape seemed to be out of the question. I couldn't imagine how I would handle the next blows. The cane swished four more times, and four red stripes colored my buttocks. For a while, he stroked my back and bottom, but my thoughts had only one goal: to get out of there.

When he took me in to the shower, he warned me not to close the door because sometimes the lock would snap shut. I left the door ajar and cooled my bottom with icy water for a while. By the mirror, I tried to freshen up my sweaty hair and smudged eyes.

In the mirror, through the slightly open door, I noticed his face as he stood in his office. He seemed lost in thought, looking a bit gloomy, maybe angry. He didn't see that I was watching him as he walked across the office, apparently thinking hard about something. Whether about himself, where he had made his mistakes, why this time everything had turned out differently, or about my reactions and behavior, I could only guess.

The smell of coffee drifting in from the kitchen didn't please me at all. I wanted to get out of there as soon as possible. I had no interest in talking over the previous hour. I concentrated; the main thing was not to cry or let him provoke me into some pointless words.

I thanked him for the coffee and poured a lot of milk into it so I could drink it fast. In the office, he appeared again the self-confident, self-assured, infallible man in his forties—whom I didn't have the least desire to talk to any more. He tried to begin a conversation, but the result was a monologue accompanied by shrugging my shoulders or an indefinite nod.

I drank my coffee and asked him to take me back to my car. He stood up and locked the office—but in the hall he blocked the approach to the front door with his hand. I shrank away in shock. He stroked me and, with an overconfidence that was incomprehensible to me, told me that next time it would be better, that I wouldn't be so afraid but that I would enjoy it, and that we would arrange it all by e-mail. If I hadn't been in a strange neighborhood about twenty kilometers away from my car, I would have lost control of myself and told him something about his arrogance. But instead I just set my teeth and went outside.

In the car, he didn't broach the topic, surprisingly. He talked about where he would go fishing on the weekend and about problems that he had been dealing with lately at work. I listened with only half an ear. I didn't even feel my painful bottom; I just measured the kilometers by my eyes. When I saw the parking lot with my car, that was a load off my mind. He parked beside, and I just said goodbye briefly and got out of there. He waited til I had backed out.

As I drove away, I watched in the mirror to make sure he wasn't following me. When I was sure that he wasn't, I drove into a side street among family houses, propped my head on the steering wheel, and cried for maybe half an hour. My emotions swung between anger at myself, anger at him, sorrow, and hatred, until I calmed down a bit and was able to continue driving.

Once at home I saw my bottom, all full of colors, and realized fully how much it hurt. The next day, I wrote an e-mail—but probably not the sort he was expecting. I saved it without sending, wanting to think it over yet. The following day, I toned down the text a bit, deleted and supplemented parts, but again didn't send it. That evening I found an e-mail from him—as I expected, full of questions—but surprisingly, Mister Infallible had found mistakes on his side too. It would make no sense to send off my prepared text now, and I didn't feel like writing a new one. I canceled my massage and some other activities I'd had planned.

The marks were slowly disappearing, and I was coming to realize quite clearly that the pain wasn't the thing that bothered me most about that evening. His behavior wasn't that of natural authority; he wasn't able to engross me. With his figure he aroused only fear and respect.

In his next e-mail, surprisingly, he expressed his concerns about whether I was sick or what has happened, that I wasn't writing. I still wasn't sure how to formulate my letter as aptly as possible, and so I didn't write anything yet. It was the same the next week. After I put my thoughts in order—that he didn't know my real name or where I lived or worked—I didn't send any answer. He wrote about three more e-mails and several texts, but after that I stopped hearing from him.

Some time later, I made another attempt through an advertisement, but just a correspondence one; the person in question only wanted to exchange e-mails. He didn't want a face-to-face encounter; he didn't exclude it, but he preferred just writing. He wrote beautiful, long e-mails, full of fantasies and also real experiences. Our correspondence became regular—and I didn't want any other reality. The e-mails of Mister Infallible passed out of my mind, thanks to a large number of new ones. I didn't delete them, but their meaning lost sense.

It was springtime. After a long winter, finally the first sun. Every day I was holding calls at work, answering emails, and dealing with clients. The office was quite busy. Some clients were invited to a meeting by my two coworkers—and when the door opened who should appear but *him*—the man from that disastrous evening.

I couldn't move. I was in a cold sweat, and my heart was pounding. My mind was racing: was this an accident or a deliberate maneuver? He didn't show a sign of recognition, not even batting an eyelash. He gave me, as he would any other client, folders with papers and a request to look through them and submit a report to him. With that, he said goodbye. I was thankful to him for the quick meeting and hoped that my coworkers hadn't noticed my abstractedness.

I went away to change into clean underwear and a dry blouse. I would have to wring out the clothes I'd been wearing. Once again, I appreciated my longtime habit: it's always worth having a change of clothes at the office—and not just for when you spill coffee on yourself.

In my own office, I opened the folders. The first two were just full of company papers, but the third one, handwritten, belonged just to me.

It contained a request and an instruction at the same time. He wrote that many questions remained unanswered, and so he asked that I devote the time of today's lunch break to him. He told me that he would be waiting in his car, one street behind my company's building. I appreciated that everything had gone without a hitch at the office, even thought his message seemed a bit uncouth to me.

There was no time for a long debate. I told my coworkers that I was not going to lunch with them and that maybe I would be a bit late. I took my coat and left the building.

He was waiting where he'd said. The car door were ajar, and I got in and just stared in amazement. A nice, attractive, man, suntanned from the mountains, was asking me whether we would go for lunch or what was my wish. I had the collywobbles. I would hardly be able to get lunch down, so I chose coffee.

He was full of compliments about how wonderful I looked in the suit and with shorter hair. He drove outside the town, and soon turned onto a cart track. I came back to earth. I was saying to myself, *What did you expect from him?* But I got another shock. He took out two coffees, bought just before at the gas station, and a bottle of water. He explained to me that now, at noon, he didn't think we would find any restaurants where we would be undisturbed, and that he would like to use the half hour for an uninterrupted talk.

My shock and nervousness eased a bit, but still I was on my toes. For a long time, he didn't want to reveal how he found me, but he'd had one clue, my license plate number, that I hadn't realized. With help of an acquaintance, he had found out the name of the car owner and, step by step, a bit too complicatedly, also other personal data. It had taken him quite long, but because I didn't answer e-mails or texts, he had no other way. He confessed that several times in the afternoon and in the evening, he had tried to wait behind the house where I live, but he didn't catch me going in or out, and he didn't want to ring. So he had decided on a visit to my office.

Time was flying incredibly fast; the lunch break was over. He looked even better than he had that time in the shopping center. Easy, pleasant behavior, no big-headed gestures … It occurred to me that he might have a twin brother, because the change was noticeable in every sentence that he spoke. My fear of some reproaches was totally unfounded, and returned to the topic of our meeting several times, there wasn't any criticism, either from his or my side. He conceded some disappointment, and my guessing that back then he had been angry mainly with himself, proved to be true.

I would have listened to him for a long time yet, but time was unstoppable, and I had to get back to work. Still he didn't fail to comment that for not writing at least a few lines, I would deserve twenty-five. Laughing, I accepted the offer, that sometime I would certainly take him up on that. He nodded and impudently added that after the experience with e-mails, he wouldn't put the thrashing off too long.

Suddenly, his words were pleasant to me; they sounded tantalizing. To his astonishment, I agreed. I got out of the car and took my jacket off. He sat at a nearby tree stump, gave me his hand, and bent me over his knee. He hiked my short skirt up above my waist, and his leather belt landed regularly on my stuck-out bottom. The blows were probably a bit smaller than back in the gym, but they still stung and hurt a lot. With two short pauses in between, I counted twenty-five. He stroked both my buttocks and whisked me back to work.

Since then, I've answered his e-mails regularly—and the thrashing was not the last one.

Chapter Fifteen

What If I ...

I was sitting restlessly on the subway, my eyes just wandering around. My eyes rested on a man who was hanging onto the bar above me. Lightly grizzled temples, a black winter coat, dark pants ... Quite a good-looking man. However, my eyes fell upon gleaming metal on his left ring finger. Hm, a married man ... That's interesting. But why is it so interesting? Why had the married man caught my attention? So what? In fantasy, the sky's the limit, right? What if I threw away my moral principles, personal attitudes, and I don't know what else? What if I ...

"Nice coat. Judging by the cut, it must be from Zara—but you probably don't know for sure, since your wife bought it for you." I smiled at him and moved so he could sit down next to me. "She has good taste, anyway."

"Oh, thank you. I took it as an ordinary present, so I'm glad that people like it." He didn't know how to react.

"Nice to meet you. My name is Viera."

"I'm Martin."

Interesting. When you throw away your moral principles, you don't care that he is married. It is, on the contrary, quite a turn-on. Married, a family, hm? So he must be also responsible—and it's clear they're not starving, when he has this posh coat. How long has he been under the yoke of marriage? Is he happy? And do I really care? What if I ...

"You must be on your way home from work. How about having a drink with me? Clearing our heads for a while will do both of us good. I know a good wine bar at the next stop. Just one glass—a pleasant ending to the day ... What do you think?" I asked, just by the way.

"Oh, well, you know, I … Well, why not? It'll only hold me up a little while."

So, he probably isn't such a happily married man, if he is so susceptible to persuasion. Or it isn't for the first time?

We dived into my favorite wine bar and ordered a bottle. Of course, the alcohol loosened our tongues, and we enjoyed a cheerful little talk. We had a great time together, just like old friends from school. The time flew remorselessly, and soon evening had fallen. But neither of us felt like going home; neither of us wanted to be responsible; neither of us was thinking of consequences. Nowadays, things are done too easily. The taxi drove us to a nearby hotel, and we opened the door into our room.

"Mmm, Martin, that was such a pleasant evening. Lucky it doesn't end yet …" I took off my coat and threw it on the coat-stand. Martin opened the champagne.

"Our evening is just beginning," he answered, a bit drunk with wine.

Slowly I came to him and took off his coat, slowly. I also unbuttoned his shirt and, for the first time, stroked his chest. He passed me a glass of sparkling wine, and we drank a toast to …

To what, actually? To having fun, to a nice evening, to selfish wishes and sensual desires? How lovely, how independent; the new memories will be part of the mosaics of our lives, but how will we remember them later on?

Hush, my conscience, you have no business here now.

We drank to unexpected meetings. My lips touched the cool glass of wine, and my lipstick imprinted a proof of my presence on the glass. A drop of wine lingered on my lip, and Martin kissed it lightly away. I cuddled him, and we started to kiss longingly. The glasses were laid aside, and our clothes soon followed them. Our naked bodies fell on the bed in a tangle.

I don't even know how, but suddenly I found myself in a strong hold in his lap. At first I didn't know what was going on, but the first smack made it clear to me. Actually, I knew exactly what was going on.

"Ouch! What are you doing?" I yelled with a pretend-scared look.

"Don't tell me that, with your character, you don't belong among women who like this." He didn't stop spanking me.

"Ouch! Well, I don't know—ouch—no one has ever spanked me—*ouch!*—especially not before sex," I answered untruthfully. Of course I did like thrashings—especially before sex.

"So welcome to the premiere," he smiled through the mist of alcohol.

First I made a lot of fuss; I tried to negotiate and defend myself with talk of women's rights (*hm, woman's rights; that's interesting, just now…*), but my light resistance aroused him even more, and my bottom soon changed to the same color as the rosé that we had shared in the bar. Then, of course, I also started to enjoy it—and I remembered the conversation we'd had as we were drinking the wine.

"You all claim that women are beautiful, so tell me: what is the most beautiful thing about us?" I asked playfully.

"The most beautiful feature is, of course, a female bottom," Martin answered cheerfully.

So he was an ass-man; great.

"Hmm, so, the bottom … Then which kind? The one nicely tight in close-fitting pants, or the one inconspicuously hidden in a skirt, waiting for someone to find it and show it to the world?" I continued to test him.

"What could such a bottom do in this world?" He played into my hands.

"Well, if that happened and it were to look at the wide world, then it should have a pretty good view—and, as is well known, the view is best from a male lap, right?"

"Hm, a very interesting theory indeed," he answered mock-scientifically.

Was I was already planning how the evening would end up, even then? Or earlier still? Anyway, there was no time for considerations like that now, because my bottom had already exceeded the color of the good rosé, and I was slowly getting closer to the threshold between excitement and pain. He probably sensed it, because from time to time he stopped and stroked my bottom—and slowly he also worked his way into my feminine crevice, which was already bountifully ready for him.

He helped me to stand up, bent me forward over the bed, and started pushing rhythmically into me—never forgetting to keep my bottom in a suspense. We lay down on the bed, and he put me on my back, placed a pillow under my pelvis, lifted up my legs, and again entered me with no problem. My buttocks were now ready again, and he warmed them with his vigorous touch; meanwhile, my "little shell" was delighted from the inside. I was thrusting my hips to him, and at the same time I tried to dodge the smacking spanks.

What is his wife probably doing right now? Is she making the dinner like a model wife and waiting for him? Kids running around and not wanting to take a bath? Or is she out with a friend, maybe just in the restaurant next door, enjoying trading stories of their husbands? He should have been home by now; is she worried? Or did he send her a message with some excuse?

Again, you morality, get lost, shoo; I'm enjoying this. What if I ...

One position was not enough for us; our bodies intertwined in different sexual positions, but every time his hand found a way to make contact with my bottom. My bottom was turning red, my desire intensified, my climax was coming closer ... And suddenly—the end. It was over. The spanks ceased, the contractions slackened, the excitement faded, and each of us lay on either side of the bed ...

I was wakened up from my dream by the man with the wedding ring standing above me.

"Darling, we're getting off. Jane wrote me already, asking where we are, and telling me that the grandchildren can't wait."

He grasped my hand and helped me to stand up—which came in handy to me. I still had a bit of a sensitive bottom after our last night, after all. You know, a holiday nest offers opportunities for our play ...

Chapter Sixteen

A Wife And A Housemaid

The broom swished through the air and a punished housemaid cried desperately. She was getting a spanking from me for the first time. I expected that she would get many beatings more before she learned not to forget things that she should do. I was whipping her bare bottom, and watching my wife sitting opposite me. She was smiling because she had no idea that soon she would get a beating too. It seemed that she liked the thrashing the housemaid was getting, lying over my knee with her skirt hiked up. When she had her naked bottom nicely stuck out and blow after a blow landing on it, she would groan in the same way as the maid now did.

For the last several years, I'd gone to a summer residence in a village close to the mountains. I lived there with the family of a local teacher, and soon I fell in love with his oldest daughter. A few months ago, we got married and I took her to the city. The day before our departure, my new mother-in-law gave some last advice to the bride about the cooking and cleaning. My wife said that she didn't have to worry because she knew how to cook and clean. However, I said that I would have a housemaid for that.

"A housemaid?" the mother-in-law said.

"What housemaid?" my wife asked.

"Anyone that you wish, darling," I told my wife, whose eyes lit up as she ran out of the house.

In a moment, she brought a self-conscious blushing girl, whom I recognized as one of her bridesmaids.

"Could it be Ann?" my wife asked.

"She is a daughter of a local shoemaker," said the mother-in-law. "She is friends with Jaruška. Ann has five sisters, and her parents will be happy that one of them is able to take care of herself."

"Can you cook?" I asked.

"Yes, sir." The girl nodded her head energetically.

"All right," I said. "In the afternoon I will visit your parents, and if they agree, you will go with us tomorrow."

Jaruška flung her arms round my neck and Ann thanked me diffidently.

Ann´s parents agreed and so my wife had a housemaid. She knew how to cook, and at first she was very conscientious. However, after about four months, she started to be untidy. From time to time it happened that, when I came home from work in the afternoon, I found the housemaid sitting and chatting with my wife in the kitchen, while the dishes went unwashed. I told my wife to look after the housemaid, and, for a few days, everything was in order. When it happened again, though, I got angry and gave the maid a good telling off. So when I came home one evening, two weeks later, and found a waste bin full of trash standing in the kitchen while the maid was talking cheerfully with my wife, I flew into a rage.

"Take a knife and a piece of string and come with me," I commanded the maid.

We went into the park to a robust birch tree. I sat down on the bench and commanded the maid to cut ten twigs and bring them to me. I stripped the leaflets, chose eight of the same length, and told her to give me the string. While I was tying the stronger ends of the twigs with the string, the maid asked, "I´m going to get a beating, sir?"

"You know what I´m doing?" I asked.

"That´s gonna be a broom, sir. My cousin used to get a spanking with it when she was very naughty." "And have *you* ever gotten a beating?" I asked.

"I have, sir. Our father used to thrash us with a belt," she said and lowered her head.

When the broom was done, she asked quietly, "Why am I going to get a beating, sir?" "Because you are messy. You didn´t take out the trash again."

"I forgot," she said and a tear glistened on her face.

"Why did you get a beating at home?" I asked.

"Because I misbehaved or didn´t obey, sir."

"And when you got a thrashing with the belt, did it hurt?" I asked.

"Ohh, it hurt! Then I was very, very good!!"

"Well see, when you get a beating today, you won´t forget to take out the trash tomorrow," I said, giving her the broom, and we went home

There were two neighbors standing in front of the house, chatting. When the maid saw them, she tried to hide the broom behind her back, but that only caught the neighbors' attention. The maid blushed with shame and quickly ran into the house. The neighbors smiled and one of them said, "They both deserve twenty-five blows, Doctor."

I stopped in astonishment. We had just one maid. It was obvious that she would get a beating thanks to the broom that she was holding. Twenty-five would be a punishment proportionate to her wrongdoing, and to really hurt, she must get a thrashing on her naked bottom. But what did the woman mean by "both"? Only when I reached home did it occur to me that the second one was supposed to be my wife. The neighbor was a local advocate's widow and a very smart lady. I always valued her opinion, and if she advised this, I should do it.

The broom was lying on the table in the kitchen, and the maid had taken out the waste bin. Too late—for her and also for my wife. When the maid got back, I called her into my room. I withdrew the chair from the table and leaned my left leg on it. Then I commanded her to bring the broom. She obeyed. She came and stood in front of me with the broom in her hand. She went weak at the knees, and tears were rolling down her red cheeks. Just why that was, my wife realized only when I bent the maid over my knee and hiked up her skirt. My wife started to say something, but when a white behind appeared under the maid's skirt, she changed her mind and watched with interest to see what would happen next. Then, all of it went quickly. I took the broom from the maid's hand, wrapped my arm firmly round the maid's waist, and started whipping her bottom with the broom. The broom swished through the air; the housemaid squealed with pain and swung her arms as her bottom slowly turned red. It didn't take long before I had counted twenty-five. Before I let her go, I asked my wife to bring a knitting needle. I fastened the maid's skirt with it so that it stayed hitched up. Then I took the maid into a corner of the room, where she had to stay with her bottom bared and her hands behind her head.

"The reason is that you won't forget today's thrashing for a long time," I said. "And if you move before I allow you to, you will get more blows."

I took my wife by the hand and led her into the bedroom. She went gladly, having no idea what was waiting for her there. I closed the door, put my finger on her mouth, and silently opened the door again. The maid rubbed her bottom vigorously. When she heard me, she quickly moved her hands back behind her head and started to cry again. At that moment, I felt sorry for her, but she had to learn to be obedient. I came to her, bent her forward with my left hand and, with my right one, smacked her on her bottom. It must have hurt a lot, and I was sure that now she would be afraid to move. I didn't want her to know that the madam would get a beating too.

When we reached to the bedroom, I asked my wife to give me her hairbrush, and I sat on the bed. When she brought it, I took her by the hand and put her across my lap. She realized that she was to get a beating when I began hiking up her skirt. She burst into tears and started to resist. To no avail—I was holding her firmly. But she was wearing so many underskirts that I wasn't able to bare her bottom. I let her go. She jumped up and started yelling at me, red with anger. I didn't listen to her; I just said, "Take your skirt off. You will get a beating just as the housemaid did."

She didn't obey me and wanted to leave.

"Take the skirt off, or I will call the maid to bring the broom!" I commanded her.

She began to beg and make promises.

"Take the skirt off immediately or I will call the maid, and, not only will you get a spanking with the broom, but she will also watch it!"

Slowly and unwillingly she started taking her clothes off. I felt more and more like thrashing her. When the skirt and underskirts were finally removed and she was standing there in front of me in her panties, I nodded to her. She obeyed and came closer. I untied the lace on her panties and let them fall to the ground. Then, I put her across my lap again. Her bottom was white just as the maid's had been, and in a while she would hers would be the same red color. I took the hairbrush and, for the first time, smacked her on her bottom with it. A red stain appeared right away, and my wife screamed with pain. I smacked her the second time, and my wife started shrieking. I took her by her hair and made her to kneel.

"If you are going to rage like this, the maid will realize that you are getting a beating even when she doesn't see it," I said.

"It hurts so much," sobbed my wife.

"You are getting a thrashing—it must hurt. And before you get twenty-five, it will hurt a lot more. Put your head under the pillow and then groan as loudly as you wish. It's enough that the whole house has heard that the maid got a beating; they don't have to know that I had to punish you too!"

She obeyed and covered her head with the pillow. After that, only the smacks of the hairbrush landing on her bottom and weak sobs muffled by the pillow could be heard. I didn't spare her at all. The brush landed alternately on her right and left buttocks. I was holding her firmly so she couldn't slip out of my grasp. She swung her arms and legs but kept her head under the pillow. The fear of shame was stronger than the pain that she had to undergo. When the brush landed for the twenty-fifth time, her bottom was red like a love apple. She got up quickly, grasped her stinging bottom with both hands, and started to skip in the bedroom. Tears were rolling down her cheeks as she sobbed quietly. I watched her and smiled. The maid would need a few more thrashings before she learned everything, but my wife would not. I was sure that, for her, today's thrashing was a sufficient lesson.

Chapter Seventeen

Bodyguard III

Finally, I was looking forward to an undisturbed evening at home, sitting in the armchair, with a martini. Lately, we had many things going on—concerts, interviews, finishing the new record. Lily and I spent evenings at concerts, in studio, and when we were lucky, so also in bed. With luck, we would fall asleep after sex and not before it. So I really liked the idea of a free evening and a long sleep.

But just when I entered my apartment, it was clear to me that nothing would go according to plan. I felt her in here, and I smelled her perfume—I would recognize it even in a perfumery. It was simply Her. But today, she had written me that we wouldn't see each other in the evening because she had something going on. "What's happening *again*?" I thought.

"Hey, honey," I said as I took off my coat in the hall.

Silence. Silence is not a word that goes with Lily, so, curious, I entered the kitchen, which was connected to the living room. The space felt big, which erased the fact that, otherwise, it was quite a small apartment.

The look of a savage dragon would be a fervent expression of the deepest love compared with the look Lily gave me. She was standing behind the bar which connected to a kitchen countertop, which enabled a man (women forgive) to keep a woman company while she cooked. She was wearing black tube dress pulled below her knees and elegant black pumps. Along with her relatively classic makeup and discreet braid gave the impression that she was a normal girl. But something was wrong here; something was definitely wrong. Otherwise, she wouldn't cast lightning at me.

"Darling, what´s the matter? I—" I started to say.

"Whose are?" she barked at me.

"Whose are what? I don´t know what—"

She held up a lacy black G-string and she threw on the bar..

"So you already know whose they are?" Lily said. "I found them in the couch between the cushions." She shot me with more lightning.

"Lily, I really don't know. I … I have never seen them. This is absurd, I …" I was drowning in my own sweat.

"I want to hear the truth. Then, I will be able to leave with grace and without a scene," Lily uttered with cool composure. If she had had a weapon, I would have already been beyond the veil.

On the other hand, my composure had left quite quickly, and I was panicking. Do you know the feeling when in one minute, you have a great life, a beloved girl, a job that you like, and in the next, everything comes apart at the seams? Well, I do, and I wouldn't wish it on you.

"Lily, please, I really don't know … It's not what it looks like." Gosh, another embarrassing cliché. How should I tell her that it was true, that I didn't have a woman in here, that I hadn't seduced anyone, that I didn't take the G-string off anyone? This was like a bad dream. "I didn't have any woman in here. I wasn't cheating on you, not here and not anywhere else," I said. "God, Lily, you have to believe me." Did she have to? I felt sick. Of course she didn't have to believe me. How would I feel if found men's briefs in her room? There are things that are really hard to explain, but now, there was nothing to explain. My hands were clean. "I really have no idea whose G-string this is or how it got here." I was desperate, my adrenaline was up, I wanted to catch her and shake her so she would wake up and believe me, I wanted to start shouting that I wasn't cheating on her, I wanted to …

"OK, so then I can put them on again," she said. And with a smile like the Virgin Mary, she pulled the G-string on over her pumps.

I wanted to warm her bum …

"I wanted to know how you would react and if you would, by chance, fall for the bait and tell me, without pulling any punches, something about your possible lover," I explained to him. He was standing there like an idiot trying to recover from the shock. "Don't tell me that it wasn't a good idea to stir you up a bit and find out how you were doing. I've been bored lately. Not at work, but in bed. We never have enough time or strength for more complicated or longer foreplay, so why not at least a fine quickie? To bring up the idea of cheating and not turn a hair, for that I should praise myself and win an Oscar. That scared look when you thought that you would lose me, that I will remember for a long time yet. You were really sweet. I love you."

"What? You're giving me a heart attack insinuating that I'm unfaithful, that … that you will break up with me, and you explain it like this?" On the other hand, it was good bait. If I did have some lover in the wings, I would probably have gotten caught in the trap. The corners of my mouth started twitching.

"Oh yeah, and I still have forty-eight minutes to make up for it," she said, smiling like butter wouldn't melt in her mouth.

"Come here." I nodded toward the armchair, where I sat down and got comfortable. I bent that minx of mine over my knee and started thrashing her cunning bottom. I don't know what I wanted to beat more, the two beautiful buttocks smiling at me as I freed them from under her dress or the damned G-string, which surely gave me my first gray hair. Anyway, soon, because her bottom was so red, I started to impair the image of the black beauty. Lily was smiling and teasing me. On purpose, she turned her bottom away, and then did the opposite, she complied with my wishes. She kicked her little legs, stroked my leg, then again banged on the armchair. She was enjoying it, and I didn't let her provoke me very much. With every smack I forgot about the shock and panic and got on the same wavelength as my love.

"You were sweet, standing there totally destroyed and thinking feverishly about how the panties got there." Lily was having a good time, and she sighed lightly from time to time.

"I'll teach you, sweet," I said. "In a while you will remember me as the one who warmed your bum without panties." I pulled hers down and threw them across the room. I went on mapping the beautiful surface of those two hemispheres in my lap, being overcome with new feelings after the recent experience. My pants started to get a bit tight, and Lily shifted her position so she could also satisfy herself on the other side of the hemispheres.

"I will remember you as the one who made love to me just before dinner with my papa," she said when I stopped. She gave me a wink. Oh, I see, dinner with papa. So now I understand her conservative clothing. Her conservative daddy would allow nothing else.

I helped her stand up, unzipped her dress, and let it slip down to her ankles. At the same time, Lily unhooked her the black bra and threw it across the room. In all her beauty, Lily slipped out of her pumps and bent over the armchair. I just couldn't help myself w and I smacked her bottom several more times. But it's true that I started to be more interested in her moist little shell, which I lightly dove into several times that evening. Later we lay next to each other in bed—we ended up there after our love traveled through the apartment—nestled together just like that. I felt wonderful, and I think that Lily too. This was exactly what we needed. The unsuccessful event of last month shifted forever into a distant memory. Lily looked at me as if she was reading my thoughts. "We are together again, just like we used to be, right? I love you, Jeremy."

"I love you too, Lily," I answered with a smile. Then I buried myself in memories.

It was too much for of us. We were swallowed up by work and there was no time left for our relationship. Once, Lily came to my apartment and before she got in the door, she was yelling like one possessed that I didn't do anything, that I didn't care about anything, that I couldn't be relied on, that such-and-such was missing, and when will this or that be done, and will I will watch it and arrange it. I never minded that my love was at the same time my boss, that she paid me and employed me. I didn't have a problem with my salary, but I definitely didn't like the fact that she took her work home. Instead of making use of the free evening when we could be together, she just yelled at me like a street sweeper. She could do this at work, and we could have words with each other about work, but this was too much for me. I knew that I had a lot of those things that she was barking at me about under control and I knew when, how, and especially why they would be done. But as I said, we should have solved this at work. I laid aside my martini, which had turned bitter in my mouth. I went to Lily, took her firmly by the hand, and pulled her over to the armchair, where I bent her over my knee.

"Jeremy, stop! You can't do this!" she barked.

"Why? You need to cool down. You're behaving like a silly goose." I smacked her on the beautiful booty for the first time, which was rounded under her leggings and a long T-shirt, which wasn't long enough to be a dress, at least according to my criteria.

I thrashed her regularly, but I let her speak.

"Jeremy, you don't have the right to beat me now. I'm your boss, remember ..."

"Well yes, you are, but at work, not at home. At home we are partners, remember." I didn't let her finish, and I tried to subdue my growing anger.

"That doesn't matter. Before the tour, I can give work orders to you any time I want to," she answered unpleasantly.

"Really? Hardly. At work, want what you want and I will work hard, but when we are at home, I would appreciate calm time together without quarrels, Lily."

"OK, get stuffed!" She started resisting the spanks. "You know what, Jeremy? I can easily fire you." She thought that she had a trump.

I let her go. "Yes, that you can, Lily," I answered calmly, helping her up. We cast a look at each other.

"All right, you're fired." As soon as she pronounced the words, she regretted them immediately, but her pride wouldn't allow her to take them back right away.

Quietly, I got up and dialed the number of one on my security agencies and asked for a capable bodyguard.

"Tomorrow at nine in the morning, your new bodyguard Ricky will come to your office. I know him, he is capable. He was my student. If you are not satisfied with him, I'll find you another one. Now, please, give me some time to search for a new job." I showed her that I wanted to be alone. Lily angrily grabbed her purse and left. On the way to the door she stroked her bottom, which must have been pretty warm now. I would have preferred if her nice company warmed my heart and this evening had never happened. I stayed alone, with only the martini on the table to remind me of my desire for a pleasant evening.

The quiet household was a paradise compared to what happened in the following days. Lily smiled not only didn't smile at me, but she didn't smile at anyone else. She was unpleasant and uncompromising; nothing was good enough for her. Lily told Ricky off because she was not satisfied with any idea for concert protection. I tried to build up my energy, rest, get my things in order, well, not in the closet, but at least in my mind. I felt lonely. I was alone. Moments with Lily were cold. Even her kiss felt cold and her look chilled me. When I tried to speak about it, she changed the topic or went to another room, saying that she didn't want to speak about it. It couldn't go on like this.

It couldn't go on like this, that was clear to me, but I didn't know how to get out of it, except for apologizing to him and asking him to be my bodyguard again and telling him that I wanted everything to be like it was before. But you know me, I just couldn't do it. I put an icy mask on and called things my way. But my heart hungered for his presence. At work, I missed him so much, and the moments we spent together were just different. I know, all I had to do was just apologize right that evening and explain that I was just overworked and that I was very sorry, that I didn't want him to leave, that I didn't want any other bodyguard, that I want just him, and so he shouldn't be angry at me anymore. I should have explained that I wanted him to warm my bum even more and make love to me and, in the morning, we could go together to work again. That little would have been enough. Maybe I should have been like this. Maybe this was a relationship test; maybe, it was a test of my maturity. Was I able to admit my mistakes and face consequences? I had to, that I knew, otherwise it would be definitively an end and I would lose my boyfriend. I sighed deeply, resolutely took one thing out of the closet, and went to his place.

When I unlocked the door, my hands were shaking. Yes, he let me have keys still.

"Jeremy, are you here?" I tried to look calm.

"Yes." He tried to look amiable.

I didn't want to drag it out. "Jeremy, I'm very sorry for your firing and for the whole scene. I'm asking you very much to come back to me." I put a new employment contract and a pen on the table and continued, "It's exactly the same as the original one. I think that if I raised your salary, you would take offense that I'm bribing you. If I reduced your responsibilities, you would feel underemployed, so I'm offering a different compensation." I put a cane next to the pen and quietly sighed.

You have no idea how much I was relieved when she apologized to me. How gladly I would sign the new contract right away, and how gladly I would make love to my sweetheart, but it couldn't be done as quickly.

Questioningly, I looked at the cane and then at Lily. I knew very well how much she hated the cane; we had tried it just once, and after three blows, she showered me with swear words and complained that she really didn't have what it takes, that it was too much.

"How come so suddenly, Lily?" I was taking my time.

"You know what a nitwit he is," she said, trying to lighten the atmosphere. "I treat him like a dog and he dances to my tune. He tolerates everything. He is all like, 'Yes, miss, of course, miss, I'll make it, miss.' I'm not curious about that at all. With you, I could talk to you and always find the best solution. You know how to cut me down to size and discourage me from silly things; you just have a way with me, and you know a lot about your job. Please come back to work, and come back to my arms." She lowered her eyes and looked sadly at the ground.

"Are you serious?"

"Of course. Organizing doesn't go well without you while, I—"

"I mean the cane," I interrupted her.

"Yes," she answered quietly. "If it is supposed to be a thrashing for my mistake and arrogance, then it should probably be worth it." I could tell from her eyes that she was fighting with fear.

"Well, OK, take off your clothes and get ready on the bed." I had to accede to the rules so that the whole situation could be forgotten. She went to get ready, and I, with a smile, watched the city from my window. Finally everything was how it should be. I signed the contract and went to the bedroom. She was lying naked on the bed, a pillow inserted under her pelvis, another under her head, to muffle her cry and curb her tears.

"I will end when I consider the punishment sufficient." I swished the cane through the air and watched the wave of twitching that flew through her body. "If *you* wish to end the thrashing, say 'stop,' but it will not be completed—and then, choose when we will continue. You can leave any time," I told her the rules. She agreed quietly and buried her head in the pillow.

Already the first blow was flying through the air to its victim.
Ouch! How I hate the thin bitch. I have what I wanted.
I have no idea how many she will get. But she deserves it, that's true.

A second sharp blow.
Ouuuch! Already two welts decorate my bottom, and I don't even have an idea how many there will be yet. It hurts, damn.
Such a tempo, that's nice. I have to be careful; it's a dangerous tool, and I don't want to injure her.

A third meeting of the cane with the girl's bottom.

That really hurts, but he's giving me time for a rest. I'm so stupid; I could have brought a wooden spoon, but that would, with the apology, be more like ridicule.

Well, she's already managed three; let's see how brave she is.

A fourth stripe.
Now, that's my maximum—ouuch!
After the fifth blow, I'm going to change sides. Poor girl; she carries on bravely.

A fifth blow. Her body contended again with the wave of pain, and the pillow absorbed her tears.
God, I won't sit now for a long time—but I do deserve it; I'm a goose.
She won't sit for a long time now—but she does deserve it, my darling.

A sixth sharp whizz cut the air.
A loud ouuch slips out of my mouth. I don't want any more, no more, it hurts a lot. My God, Jeremy, don't torture me long! I felt like yelling; the pain is stronger than me. He would stop, but it wouldn't be finished ...
So she has already started singing, my little girl. We'll see much she can stand.

A seventh red stripe landed on the penitent bottom. "Ouch!" she howled into the pillow and pressed her buttocks tightly together, as new stripes appeared.
I'm an idiot; the cane never again, never.
How much I would like to stop. But I know that I would degrade her.

An eighth blow. She was already weeping silently and writhing on the bed. Her bottom tightened in pain, and it took some time before it slackened.
I will remember that for a long time; I'm sure about that. I don't want any more, enough. I'm reformed already, really ... No, go on, I deserve more.

She is crying. But if I stop too early, it won't have the educational and apologetic effect that she needs. I admire that she worked up the courage for solving the situation this painfully.

Three more times, three red stripes stretched over her stuck-up bottom. "Ouuuch, ouuch!" She buried her face in the mattress, and it was quite hard to remain lying down.

I will be good, really good; I will never fire him arrogantly again, never! I promise!

Every blow hurts me more than her, but I can't stop yet.

The first ten were completed. Lily bent backward and gave a cry of pain. "Stop" was hanging on her lips, but she was hard on herself; she knew that it was she who had chosen it.

Every blow burns like fire! My bottom is burning, and my whole body is twisted tight like a spring. I'm afraid of another blow, I'm afraid of the pain, I'm afraid that I won't manage it. I have never been given such a hard thrashing.

Just ten blows, but with such a sharpened bugger! It is biting into my Lily's bottom so naturally that it's hard to believe how much it must hurt.

Eleven. She was shivering with sobs and with pain, her muscles tight and bottom feverishly hot. She was clutching a pillow under her face as she tried to control herself.

Please, that's enough, please! No more, no more ...

We are probably getting closer to the limit. She wouldn't be satisfied with herself is she didn't touch it. It rends my heart, but there is no other way ...

Four quick blows completed fifteen. Lily wasn't expecting that; she shouted at the first two blows, and the next two were drowned in a loud cry. But she didn't say "stop."

Hell must feel like this. I deserve it.

I will not give her more; I can't. But she wants more.

Sixteen.

No! Nothing else was running through my mind; I was swallowed up by pain.

She won't say it; that I know for sure.

Seventeen.

"This is the last one, my love." I finished it. She was shaking, crying, sobbing into the pillow, curled into a ball.

I love him.

I love her.

Yes, everything was already as it used to be. I kissed my beloved on the forehead. "I have to go; I'm going to take a shower and powder myself. We'll see each other tomorrow in the hall, all right?"

She smiled with her eyes and kissed me.

"Sure, boss," I teased her.

Chapter Eighteen

A Present

After we graduated high school, my group of friends and I landed jobs in the same company. We four wacky high-school graduates deviated from the normal, peaceful functioning of the company's mostly older employees. Each of us got a job in a different department. Jane, thanks to her very good knowledge of English and a partial knowledge of German, started as a secretary. Denise, who was the only one with a technical knowledge, was in the development department. I was faced with business affairs, and Eva contentedly did bookkeeping. We had a lot of fun and also some troubles. After three years, Denise invited us to her wedding and informed us that she was expecting a baby. I don't know if she inspired us, but the fact was that within two years, each of us had a beautiful healthy baby. We left the babies in the care of their fathers or grandmas and kept going out alone as we used to. This idea became a tradition, and we celebrated all name days and birthdays together. The dates were divided relatively equally through the whole year, and so every month or two, there was a reason to call the hen party, discuss new gossip, and give presents. It changed from giving individual trifles to contributing to a collective present. Cosmetics were followed by jewels, scarves, shawls, or belts, until Eva suggested a change with the arrival of the New Year. I claimed a woman never has enough jewelry and accessories, but the others were enthused by the suggestion of the group gift. The originator of the idea took charge of ensuring the first gift. There wasn't much time left, and so at the January get-together, Jane got a chocolate massage for her birthday. All three of us participated in inventing and securing following gifts. Eva contended with an unpleasant allergy every spring, and so, for her birthday in February, she got a permanent pass to a salt cave, which was supposed to ease her problems. Fortunately, my fear of getting presents for crazy or adrenaline-filled activities, like bungee jumping or zorbing, wasn't realized. At the beginning of March, we got a free ticket for a daylong HEAT program or the day of exercise and health for Denise, who is sports minded.. The leaflet promised a trial use of boss with flexi-bars and on special moving belts that are propelled only by muscular energy. For Jane, we managed to ensure a ticket to a well-known beauty salon, where the deft hands of a cosmetician gave her a makeover and an image consultant gave her lots of valuable advice. A preholiday meeting belonged annually to me. I celebrated my name day on the last day of June. I chose an outdoor get-together for the occasion. We didn't call the meetings during the holidays, and at the end of September the weather often didn't enable us to sit outside. I like to do exercise, but lately, the workload and laziness were winning. That gave my friends a motive for a gift. I got a permanent pass to a newly open fitness center.

I booked the first lesson, and at the arranged time reported to the reception desk. A young lady took me to a big air-conditioned room full of new machines, shining dumbbells, and fitness balls. A young man took charge of me. He introduced himself as Peter, and his body clearly showed that he spends plenty of time here. After a short conversation, he found out that my experience is minimal, and he offered me choose between the instructors working there. I chose a woman—she seemed nice in the picture, and I supposed that I would have a good rapport with her. Unfortunately, she offered just morning hours, and the criterion for my choice was, after all, the time. Late afternoon hours belonged mostly to Peter, and so it was decided he would instruct me. I changed my clothes in the dressing room, and the torture began. Warming up on the bike was okay, but all the other fitness machines were hard. He lowered the originally planned series of exercises, but still, I was hardly able to climb the stairs afterward, and my hands hurt as if I reaped a truckload of hay. I cursed my friends; the others had lazed in a massage or in the salt cave, and I hardly managed to mop the sweat from my forehead. The second lesson didn't give my trainer any better impressions, and I had to apologize for missing the third one because of business reasons. The recommended diet remained just on the paper and so, during the next visit, he made it clear to me that such an approach made no sense. He asked me dead seriously if I wanted to keep coming there, and if so, that he would recommend special classes.

I had an interest in keeping fit. Somehow, with age, I struggled with losing weight more often. And so despite the warning that it will be a stricter method, I nodded. I fight with inconsistency and laziness often, so I had no other choice.

There was the same room waiting for me and a similar schedule of exercises, and I started to think naively that it was just some kind of frightening method used to increase discipline. He wrote down thoroughly every series of exercises. Notes written in green were followed by notes written in red; the number of notes was growing.

When the lesson was over, he acquainted me in detail with the method. When I didn't perform the number of repetitions or the difficulty level or duration of exercises according to the table, there was a "reward" waiting for me. I hesitated for a moment—it was the last chance to say *no*. I did feel like doing exercise, but I knew that when I don't have any scourge above me, I look for any possible excuses and arguments to get around.

He opened a locker in the corner of the room. Scourges, bats, canes, and belts of various length and strength were hanging on hooks, perfectly in-line. A bit curiously and a bit with embarrassment, I examined the contents of the locker more closely and felt his fixed stare. He locked the locker again, we exchanged good-byes, and I left to take a shower and change clothes.

At home, I meditated for a long time whether the positive reply was the right one. He gave me the schedule of exercises, but the specific punishments for their nonperformance were not there. I made a copy of the schedule and completed it with my estimation of which series I could manage without penalty points and where problems will probably occur. I supposed that I could estimate my abilities quite well, and the result surprised me pleasantly. There were just a few red numbers of a low value. In fact, I even eliminated a few of my favorite but totally unsuitable meals from my diet and replaced them by recommended ones, of which the most edible one was a serving of cottage cheese. The rest of the new meals didn't win my affection. Due to my daily routine at work and at home and attending to other duties, I didn't have much time for thinking about the next visit to the fitness center. In the morning, I packed a gym bag, and in the evening I waited at the reception desk ahead of time. Peter had told me that he doesn't tolerate clients being late. At the reception desk, there wasn't a living soul around; I leafed through a sports magazine, looking at pictures and reading the advice of experts.

He greeted me with a smile, praising me for punctuality. At that moment, none of us realized that it was both the first praise and the last for a very long time. He made sure again that I didn't rethink my decision. He gave me a paper with a schedule for today's lesson, made sure that I hadn't inflicted a wound on myself during the week, and that I hadn't contracted any virus or cold.

I started at the treadmill, and I never expected how much criticism I would hear about the style of walking or running. On the paper, the first red notes started to appear. By the end of the lesson, it seemed that the sheet was covered in red. My naive ideas about managing individual exercises on particular machines vanished little by little. On one machine I was sitting wrongly, and in the correct position, the number of repetitions didn't seem to me so easy anymore; another time, I had my elbows too far from my body or I was standing wrongly, not to mention how I was using the dumbbells. The result was a total fiasco. I was coming to believe that it was a miracle that I'm even able to walk.

He was still smiling. I was mopping sweat and prolonging the length of breaks by drinking, tying my shoelaces, and making all kinds of possible excuses. After the final exercises and proper stretching, I sat down with relief. He passed me for inspection a paper full of red abbreviations, unreadable notes and scribbles, and the table. With another color, he started writing numbers and capital letters with a slash and a number. I had a premonition that meant the first letter of the tool and a number for its strength or length. Even thought I looked at it for a long time, I wasn't able to get my bearings in the maze of numbers and letters. But it was clear to me that there were more than enough. My homemade estimation was totally different, the reality much more cruel.

He opened the locker, put a bolster into the middle of the bench, and waited till I pulled down my sweat-drenched leggings. He warned me that tolerated this slow stripping only for the first time, and next time it will be punished. I wished to lie down, but definitely not into this position; everything hurt me. He saw that I was afraid, so he drew me close to the bench and issued an instruction on how to lie down and grip the bench by the sides. He had made no secret that most of the machines allowed very unpleasant positions for thrashings, so I shouldn't mess with him. I didn't remember the specific results I had been threatened with, so, with each tool, I was told how many blows I would get. My hands were clutching the side of the bench, and the first painful smack of the belt landed on my bottom. Bravely, I said "one," and the second blow hit my bottom. The third and fourth blows stung and hurt. I tried to hold tight, because I didn't want to be tied to the bench on any account. When I said fifteen, I got a rest. He took a short pause and stroked my buttocks several times, but I wasn't allowed to put my hands behind me. My bottom was burning and red, but there was to time to think of what would follow next. He stood up again, told me the number, tool, and what I will get for the punishment. With a sting, a smaller bat landed for the first time and then ten more times. A sensation of severe burning forced me to scratch my bottom, but immediately I got five extra blows and a strong warning.

I tried to recall the abbreviations stated on the side of the notes, so I knew what was waiting for me, but the sequence of events was so quick that I had no chance to understand all of them.

My bottom hurt. I concentrated on counting—the number of blows increased for incorrect counting—controlling my unruly hands, and not crying. I wasn't able to handle anything more.

My confused thoughts were again interrupted by a whip and a stinging pain in several places, which betrayed that he was holding scourges in his right hand. He raised his hand and struck my bottom and thighs several times. The counting was followed by moaning and wailing. Near the end, when I heard words from his, I didn't perceive the number or the tool. I only knew that the end of today's special lesson would come at any moment. After he straightened my position, a sharp pain flew through my whole body.

I screamed and released my hands—the hit by the cane was strong. He tapped the cane on the side of the bench, and I obediently put my hands back in the correct place. There were another four switches of the same intensity, another four cries of "ouch," and then finally my words of release. For a while, he stroked my bottom and explained that I myself determined the whole complementary program according to my effort and quality of exercising. At that moment, I hated his calm voice and also the constant nice smile on his face. We said goodbyes, then I took a quick shower and went back home.

At home, I went through the prepared schedule for the next lessons. It was much more variable, and there were listed several different exercises in each area. I was supposed to tick one option that was the most convenient for me. I was a long way from trying all the exercises, and so a partially new schedule formed as it had when I filled out the questionnaire. Now that I was finished preparing, I thought about each exercise and set of repetitions.

My bottom really hurt. One advantage of summer is the fine skirts and dresses I can get into get much better than into skintight jeans. Thankfully, the pain in my body and buttocks subsided relatively quickly.

A bit nervous, but with zest and a decision not to give up so easily, I waited at the lonesome reception desk for my next session until Peter invited me to enter the fitness center. He examined my plan, slightly smiled, and spoke the words: "All right."

I started to struggle with individual fitness machines in an uneven fight. I tried, I sweated, and I fought with every series of exercises with all my might. Every minute Peter added something to the schedule, and from time to time he corrected me or showed me the right rendition of the exercise. In comparison with the first session of suffering, today's lesson passed much faster. The evaluation wasn't as perfect—there were still many red notes on the paper. The table changed the marked mistakes and imperfections to penalty points. This time I knew right away what waited for me. He had written "R3/10, PD/12, R2/5."

Without stretching, I lay down on the bench, and a belt landed for the first time on my bare, sweaty bottom. I winced and hissed with pain at the same time I said "one" and whack "two," whack "three ..." My bottom was burning, but I managed the ten without getting any warning.

There was a short pause, and Peter passed his hand over my buttocks several times, but he already had a prepared beater in his hand. He straightened my back and hands and raised his hand. The first blow was accompanied by a loud smack. There was an acute, stinging pain, and then I said "ouch" and started counting. Again, there was a backswing and a loud smack, then my bottom was hot and stinging, and another red stripe appeared. I was moaning and counting, and with every new strike the pain intensified.

The cane was the most feared. There were three, and they differed in length and thickness. The middle one colored my bottom today. A searing pain flew through my body, and a first welt appeared on my buttocks. I bent with pain, but Peter's uncompromising move brought me back into the original position. The second strike was also accompanied by my wailing; I was shivering, and another red stripe appeared on my bottom. Today's lesson was resulted in five welts. For a while, Peter stroked my back and my aching behind; he helped me to stand up. and for the first time, I even heard a few words of praise from him.

I wasn't afraid of the next lesson, and I also had to confess that I was looking forward to it. But, in the morning, I overslept and quickly packed my leggings and T-shirt. At work, one problem was followed by another; when I wanted to turn the computer off in the evening and leave for my fitness class, I was held up by a long phone call. I arrived late, and Peter was sitting at the reception desk. He heard my excuse, didn't comment on it. I had left the paper with the schedule for today's lesson at home, thanks to the morning rush. While changing my clothes, he quickly made a new schedule for today. My bad morning and miserable workday were followed by a poor exercise session. The increased final sum of punishment because of my late arrival and the undelivered schedule was expected. That night, my bottom became acquainted with almost all tools placed in the locker. I was groaning. For the first time, I couldn't hold back my tears, and I cried during most of the thrashing. On my red bottom, the number of new welts and bruises was growing. I was writhing, moaning, and begging. The last strike of the cane was a relief. I was angry at myself and also at the instructor—he didn't have to be so vigorous.

My several-weeks-long vacation that began the following day, although originally planned for totally different reasons, was also a relief. I couldn't imagine myself sitting at the computer that whole day.

Pleasant lessons without punishment in the fitness center were followed by hard lessons that many times still ended with a painful thrashing.

After the last training session, instead of a sports drink, a small bottle of champagne marked the end of my first exercise program.

It's now spring; the agreed-upon break is slowly coming to an end, and I'm asking myself if I should do it again.

Chapter Nineteen

Countess

"You must be joking. What is this supposed to be? This should be a pressed tablecloth—you can't mean this seriously," she yelled at housemaids and pulled down the tablecloth. "How many times I have told you that I don't like yellow flowers?" She threw the flowers out of the vase and onto the tablecloth. "And what is this—this is supposed to be a clean vase?" The rattled housemaids sought refuge in the count, who was just coming. However, the countess continued to rage and blew up at her husband: "See, you good-for-nothing, how many times do I have to tell you to sack them? They don't know anything—they spoil everything—just look at the vase!" She flung the vase on the floor and the fragments were flying through the dining room. "So, are you going to do anything finally?" she asked.

Silence fell on the room. As the husband and wife cast their eyes at each other, the majordomo rushed quickly to prevent the catastrophe from happening. The curious servants were standing in the doorway.

"Yes, I will, as soon as I get back from my journey," he said authoritatively. He was the only one who knew that the tone was intended for his wife and not the servants. He could clearly read the question in the majordomo's eyes: "what do you want to do?"

"Please, clean it" he told the housemaids. "Please, these three days, try to make it here in peace without me," he told his wife. Then he said goodbye and left.

The countess sneaked a look at the housemaids and then went to the gardens.

The majordomo caught the count by the carriage: "Sir, I wasn't at the conflict. I'm sorry if the maids didn't do their work; I will put it in order."

"There is nothing to apologize for, my friend; I think it's me who should set things right." The young man smiled and motioned to the coachman to leave.

The count stood up for his servants; it took him a long time to find reliable people for his castle. People tried to rob him—they skimped on the food and split the extra money among themselves. He also had impudent and haughty housemaids, lazy gardeners, and drunken cooks. One day, his longtime friend advised him with an educational trick: three times and enough. Give a thrashing for a transgression, the first beating big and the second one even bigger; after the third violation, the servants were fired, and they left gladly, because the forth beating, they couldn't even imagine. And so, thieves and loafers were disappearing from his service, and the honest and hardworking ones stayed—those who were given just one sound thrashing, which was enough to them to value a decent treatment, a good salary, and a solid job. He had appointed his good friend the majordomo, and the castle was flourishing. Well, sometimes it was necessary to knock somebody into shape, but it was never a case of any serious transgression that would lead to a sound beating or firing.

He thought back to Ann. He had warmed her bum when he caught her carrying away a vase under her skirt—the vase that his wife broke today. At that time, he bent her over the table, struck her rear with a wooden spoon, and when her bottom was red, he dealt her some stinging blows with a cane. She cried and begged for compassion, but he didn't ease up. He gave Ann a good beating, and since then he has an impeccable housemaid in her. Also, Betsy was given a beating because she refused to work and she talked back to him. Her booty was also bruised properly—a belt and a cane changed a lazy girl into a diligent helper in the kitchen. And he could continue. They always had a chance to leave right after the first beating, but the motivation of having a job was stronger, and so making more trouble wasn't worth the good beating and losing a job. He didn't consider an unpolished vase or smudges on the floor serious transgression. The majordomo set it in order with a few slaps on the head and some admonishments. Although he was hesitant, he would have to use this method even on his wife. Their marriage was rather arranged, but still, he treated her with regard and respect, and he expected the same from her. However, her scene in front of the servants indicated the opposite.

"Countess, Sir is back, and he wants to talk to you in his office." The majordomo passed the message on to the young countess.

"Finally," she barked and followed the servant at a quick pace.

"You are here. About time, too. So, what are you going to do with them. Are you going to fire them all finally? I want normal servants here, I ..."

"Silence!" he said strictly. "I don't have any reason to fire my servants. They are decent people, and they serve us well. You try to find faults with them on purpose; you humiliate them, and you treat me in front of them like if I were some dandy. Therefore, I'm giving you a choice. You will either spend a week at your own castle as a housemaid to get to know their job and appreciate it, or I will punish you in the same way I would punish any other housemaid with similar behavior," he said seriously. His wife, petrified, thought he couldn't mean this seriously. She opened her mouth to shower him with objections. However, he took out a leather beater stared her into silence.

"You mean it seriously?" she asked with a timid voice.

"As a count, I don't speak in jest," he answered firmly. "So, what did you choose? Are you going to taste the life of a housemaid, or are you going to get a beating? "

"Tsk," she said as she got back her self-confidence, turned on her heel, and walked away from the office.

"If you step over the doorsill, I will take it as a choice of the first offer," the count said.

Ostentatiously, she stepped over the doorsill with a stamp.

"The countess decided to get to know your job closely. She will serve here a week just as you do, and I hope that you will accept her properly and initiate her into the work. If there is any problem, you will inform me or the majordomo. Thank you for your cooperation, and I wish you all strong nerves." The count finished his speech informing the servants about the current situation. He didn't have to worry about their cooperation during the farce that has arisen. None would dare to pay the countess back for the old wrongs. They knew how they would end up.

"Come on, get up, they are already awaiting you in the kitchen," The majordomo woke up the new housemaid in the morning. He threw new clothes on the bed and stressed the suitability of hurrying up a bit if she didn't want to have her bottom beaten up for a lack of punctuality first thing in the morning. A look from her husband, who was standing in the doorway, assured her that it wasn't a joke.

Dressed in a skirt and a blouse, and with a prideful face, she walked into the kitchen, where she was given a bowl of oatmeal and an herbal tea right away. She refused it with scorn, and so the cook started to assigned work to her—peeling potatoes! She grumbled and said that she would not bathe her hands in dirty water. However, a sharp pain across her back after being whipped by the majordomo hushed the surprised lady up.

The cook shouted, "Cut the carrot, stir the onion—don't cry—wash the bowls, and what about the pieces of broken glass on the floor?" At that moment, the majordomo was already putting things right, and her bottom was smacked with a wooden spoon. Her bottom was burning; she had blisters on her hands, a hungry stomach, and a backache from the unusual work. Her pride began to disappear, and tears formed in her eyes. She was mopping the stairs into the evenings. As her husband was passing her, she kicked the bucket with anger and doused him.

The count took the scourge from the wall and was about to punish his haughty wife. "Let me be, let me go, come on, I already got beating, enough," she pleaded as she tried to avoid the punishment.
"But not for the bucket that you spilled on me. You behave like a spoiled girl, and you rely on the fact that I, as a gentleman, will not give you a thrashing. But you are very wrong. I try to keep my position, and that is why I must bring you into line so you won't embarrass both of us," he said. And with zest, he let the strands of the scourge land on thighs of his resisting wife, who he managed to tie quickly to an armchair. In his thoughts, he thanked his father for providing him with a military training in his youth. He was heedless of her cries and gave her ten blows. He had never beaten any woman with such zest and satisfaction. When he finished, he untied her and commanded her to get back to work.

Out of her hunger, she didn't refuse supper. She then spent the evening doing the dishes. Finally, exhausted, she fell into her bed.

"I'm a countess—I can't work like this. It is humiliating—he can't dare this; he …," she said into the pillow, crying.

"You are not any countess for six more days. You are a housemaid, Helena. It was your own choice, remember? I'm giving you a chance to change your mind," her husband said as he held the leather beater in his hand again. Maybe, he even felt some pity; he knew how the day went.

Instead of a verbal answer, she looked piercingly at him.

"As you wish," he said to himself.

The next day, the shouting of the cook woke her up. "Where is she loafing? There is enough of work today" So the countess plucked the ducks' feathers, kneaded the dough, did the dishes and cleaned rooms, and picked flowers for a decoration. But, sometimes she worked slowly on purpose, or, another time, she enjoyed the sun instead of doing the work. She was always given a beating for slowness, laziness, and negligence. Sometimes she got a beating from the count; other times, it was the majordomo who discolored her bottom by giving her a stroke with the cane. When she tried to argue with him, her husband came and put things in order. At the end of the day, her bottom was nicely red, her hands were scraped from the work, and she was driven into her bed quickly from tiredness. She knew for sure that she will not make the next five days.

She was already able to appreciate the work of her servants; she knew what a hard day they had. She realized what it meant to look after the castle, and in her thoughts she admired all the people who worked there. She realized she was stupid and bossy and she really did deserve to punished. Again this evening, her husband gave her an option to choose. Only a small fireplace and a candlestick were lighting the office when she entered.

"I behaved stupidly and domineeringly; the servants are really good, they all work conscientiously and perform very good work. My behavior made the service unpleasant for them, and I'm very sorry," she said to her surprised husband.

"Are you saying that just to avoid the other days of playing the role of a housemaid, or do you really mean it?" he asked with incredulity.

"The two days of playing this role opened my eyes." She smiled. "Does the rule "three times and enough" apply to me too?" she asked quietly.

So she had learned about it.

"Yes, you should be an example to your people. Today, you will get a first—and I hope last—beating for your behavior as a countess, not as a servant." he beckoned her toward the leather armchair.

He bent her over, hitched up her smeared skirt and underskirt, and pulled her panties down. Then the countess felt another connection with her servants—she was getting spanked just as they did. After the two days, her bottom was nicely prepared, and every blow found its place. Soon, she regretted her decision to get the punishment voluntarily; every spank stung terribly. Soon, probably everyone in the whole castle knew about the beating. After eighteen blows, she was crying and yelling. She was desperate, but she knew that she couldn't withdraw from it. With each new blow, her yelling and crying intensified, and her bottom turned violet. She wanted her husband to end this suffering already, but it only ended after twenty-five blows. He untied her and helped her stand up. Now he sat in an armchair with a cane in hand and put his wife over his knee. She didn't dare to resist, but she was afraid of another spanking. With a proper whip, he landed five warning blows on her bottom to complete the punishment.

"Countess Helena, welcome back among the aristocracy," he said and kissed the back of her hand with a soft bow. "I hope that this lesson was enough for you to change your behavior toward your servants for whom, as a countess, you have responsibility, and toward me, your consort, to whom you are obliged to behave with respect and support. I don't ask you for a forced love." He took the crying woman in his arms and carried her to her bedroom and let her rest. He came back in a moment with a healing balm. She was still crying into pillows, and when he hitched up her skirt and touched her bottom, she hissed loudly and gave him a scared look.

"Not any more blows, please," he read in her eyes. Instead of an answer, he kissed her and spread her bottom with the balm.

In the morning, the housemaids came to the countess to help her with her hairstyle and clothing. She declined them with thanks. She knew how much work they had, and she was able to take care of herself. The housemaids gave each other a surprised look and left quietly. When she came down the stairs, she passed by a girl mopping the stairs. Before, she would have kicked the bucket, but now she told her good morning and enjoyed the kind answer. At breakfast, she thanked Ann for the soft pillow under her bottom. Their eyes met for a while, and they both knew that even though they were from different social classes, there was something that connects them.

Chapter Twenty

Sisters

My name is Vendula, and I have gotten thrashings at home ever since I was six. I have a sister, Barbara, who is two years younger than me, and we both used to get beaten often. We got the thrashings from our mother. Firstly, as far as I can remember, it started with several spanks by a hand over the bottom, from time to time on a bare bottom. Later when I started attending school, my mother used a wooden spoon, and again quite often on the bare bottom. At that time, of course, I hated thrashings, and I tried to avoid them by somehow lying my way out of the trouble, putting the blame on Barb, and things like that.

But later on, sometime around the age of twelve, I started finding out that I quite enjoyed thrashings in a certain way. Well, I especially liked it when I could watch Barb getting thrashed. And it didn't bother me when Barbara watched my thrashings because often, we used to get a thrashing together. Also, I often watched Barb's malicious delight when she was supposed to give our mother a spoon or prepare a chair over which I was supposed to bend as the first one to be punished. Already the thrashings had become relatively constant rituals.

When only Barb did something, our mother had it out with her alone, and I wasn't present, of course. When I wanted to see my sis get a thrashing, we had to do something together, which was quite a common case. We both gave our mother enough reasons to beat us.

Because I was the older one and usually the organizer, I usually got more. I didn't try to avoid the thrashing but rather to arrange them in a way that Barb would bear as much blame as possible. When we both got about the same thrashing, I was satisfied and felt it to be my victory. If Barb got substantially less, she felt it was her victory.

And what did the thrashings usually look like? On the last day of April when I was about fourteen and my sis was twelve, we went to a witch burning and promised our mom we would be back before 10:30 p.m. Well, we got back around midnight—and of course our mother was waiting for us. She was already in the doorway when she informed us, "So, dear girls, come immediately to kitchen so you get it over and done with quickly and you can go to bed!"

We knew right away what was waiting for us because the kitchen was where our thrashings took place. It was the ideal place because there was a drawer with spoons and a table and a chair over which we had to bend.

We both were thinking of how to put the blame on the other. It was true that Barb had wanted to go home earlier, but she didn't want to go alone, so she'd had to wait for me.

In the kitchen, after asking a few questions, mother found out that I was, once again, the main culprit. Well, I tried to equivocate a bit yet and tried to point out that I had lost sight of my sister for a while, but it was to no avail. Our mother decided I would get twenty-five spanks and Barb would get ten spanks.

"So, Vendula, stand up!" my mother addressed me. It was usual that I was the first one to get a beating.

Well, at least I would be done with it sooner.

"Vendula, give me a spoon, and you Barb, get ready the chair for her!" our mother commanded us.

From the drawer I passed her a big spoon, the one we used to always get. Barb took a chair and put it in the free space of the kitchen.

"Vendula, get ready for the thrashing!" Mother told me.

That meant that I was supposed to come and stand by the side of the chair, undo my jeans, and let them fall to the floor. Obediently I let them fall to the floor. I pulled my panties down to my knees and lay down on my stomach on the upholstered seat of the chair. My naked bottom was stuck out, and my mother took the spoon and started thrashing me with it. I had to count the blows. It smacked terribly and stung even more. My sis watched the thrashing with delight, but soon it would be her turn. I couldn't wait for the thrashing to be over. My buttocks were totally burning and red after it. Finally I rose from the chair and put my clothes back on.

"Barb, now it's your turn!" Mother said, and Barb stationed herself on my place on the chair.

I watched her humbly let her jeans fall on the floor. She uncovered her behind and lay down on the chair. Mother took the wooden spoon and gave ten blows to Barb's naked bottom.

Chapter Twenty-One

We Had an Agreement

S he was beautiful, naked in my office. Faint light from a dim lamp was reflected in her black high heels. From behind, she had a lovely silhouette: her hips, her slim waist like those of a goddess. She was standing here, in the middle of my office, with a nice view of evening New York through the window, waiting for my verdict. Can you imagine a nicer evening?

We had a rule, and she had broken it: no provocative or sexy clothes at work. Her black, close-fitting dress, a length shorter than short, was now thrown over a leather armchair. Her black undies too; yeah, the ones she got from me for her birthday. When I, her husband, had a problem retaining attention when she handed me over the records dressed like this, how could a man such as unhappily-married John, who drooled any time Alice passed by him, restrain himself? Or skirt-chaser Peter, who always leers at her? We had an agreement. She broke it.

She stood facing the window in front of my table. She had a really nice view, but I also liked mine. I was holding a long wooden ruler—a symbol of our work. Memories of times when we worked together with a pencil and a drafting table played in my mind. From behind, I laid the ruler against her neck and softly moved it along her backbone right to her bottom. I circled her buttocks and around her waist until I got to her belly. Now, I stood in front of her and stared into her gorgeous eyes, where a tear glistened. She wanted to say something. I kissed her lips. I didn't want to hear a word. We had an agreement. She broke it. Slowly, I ran the ruler over her breasts, neck, and chin. I lifted her chin and put my finger on my mouth. Not a word.

I came back to her and stood sideways. Then I swished the ruler and gave the first blow. It smacked nicely on her left buttock, and Alice jerked, her bottom shivering slightly. A real beauty. The answer to the second blow, which was a bit higher, was a soft sigh. The third—now a bit lower and with a greater force—crimped her bottom, and Alice bent backward. With the forth smack, I heard a quiet "ouch."

"Shush," I warned her. At the fifth strike, her bottom crimped and her buttocks clenched. After the sixth blow, still to the left buttock, she jerked, and her hair slipped down from a slack clip. With the seventh, again, she arched and tilted her head back. Her hair hung loose and beautiful down her back. At the eighth, she again jerked and gave a short hiss—another little red place on her lovely bottom. I didn't spare her with the ninth; I swung more strongly. She yelped as it smacked. She put her legs together and then quietly apologized and repositioned her legs slightly apart. I glimpsed a tear.

At the tenth blow—again a severe one—she managed to suppress the yell, but her whole body shivered. I went over to the other side and stroked it with the ruler. She gasped in excitement. At eleven, for a change, I hit her more moderately. After twelve, she stuck out her bottom a little more. *Oh, so you are asking for it?* I smiled and gave her three quick and quite strong blows. Every time, her body twitched, and she quivered. I gave stroke fifteen after waiting a while so she could savor it. At sixteen, the second buttock began to flush. Seventeen was a hard blow. She bent backward and clenched her butt. A sobbing "ouch" was my answer. The eighteenth lash came close after. A drop of a sweet juice rolled down her thigh.

I wanted her so much, but I couldn't neglect the rest of her punishment. Stroke nineteen was strong again. She lowered her head in her hands and sobbed. Her naked body quivered slightly, but soon she straightened up and waited for the twentieth blow. Then I commanded her to bend forward and grasp my table. Her moist shell and vulnerable butt were a big temptation. I hauled off and strongly smacked her again and again. This time I didn't give her any time to rest. Six quick blows landed; each time, she arched and hissed, but she held back her cries. She bent her little legs and tried to protect her butt with her legs close together. The table was sprinkled with her tears. She returned again to the right position, and the next two blows signaled it was not over yet.

Her quiet "please" interrupted the blows. Supposedly, she wouldn't do it again and would dress properly from now on. I would maybe even have believed her, but her naked body bent over the table—that was just a beauty. I didn't relent, and again she had first-hand experience of it. She twitched and stood on her tiptoes, her bottom crimping and groans of pain and excitement escaping her lips at more and more stinging blows.

I stopped after the thirty-fifth blow and allowed her to straighten up. I walked up to her from behind. With one hand, I slipped my fingers into her, my hand doused in her shell. With my other hand, I stroked her neck. Then once more, I commanded her to lean forward. When she heard the tinkling of my belt buckle, she began to beg for compassion. When I tenderly entered her, she just sighed with delight …

Chapter Twenty-Two

A Coach

Nowadays, it is very hard to succeed in the sports world, and if a athlete ever wants to enjoy the warmth of a precious medal in his bosom, it will cost him or her a lot of sweat, time, pain, self-denial, money, and talent. Eve was one of them. She sacrificed everything to practices and competitions—her childhood, friends, and free time. But her shelf was filled with medals and trophies. She belonged among the top performers, and all the people were looking forward to the upcoming championship. At least year's championship, she came within a whisker of taking a medal and then wept because she didn't win one. This year, she wanted to win. But something indicated exactly the opposite might happen.

"You're late," her coach greeted her harshly, which he didn't usually do. Shouting and strictness didn't have a motivational effect on her; Eva didn't belong to those people.

"Yeah, I know. I wanted to get some sleep," she answered curtly, braiding her hair. "Starting a few minutes late hasn't killed anyone yet," she thought.

"You were drinking." He drew in the aromatic air and tried to hide his disappointed look.

"Yeah, a bit. Can't we proceed with the practice? 'We're losing time."

Frustrated thoughts whirled through his head. He devoted a lot of his time, know-how, and strength to her. He didn't intend to throw everything away just for some teen excesses. He didn't intend to let her destroy everything she had achieved so far and everything that waits for her yet. She was the best of his female charges, but she could do much better. He took too much of a fancy to her.

"Today, there will be no practice. With residual alcohol in your system, I won't let you go on the parallel bars. Tomorrow, after school, I will be waiting for you here. If you come, you will accept all of my training without any protesting and bitching. I know what I'm doing. However, if you don't wanna be the champion this year, don't come tomorrow. I will pack my stuff and go somewhere else. Is that clear?" He reacted uncompromisingly. He was serious; he wasn't someone who wanted results. "She has to decide how she wants it to be," he thought.

"Okay," she said, grabbing her bag and slamming the door as she left the gym. They both knew that they would meet the next day, and they both were clear that the practice would be worth it. But their ideas of what that meant were different.

Eve got some sleep, calmed down, and went to practice after school the next day. Of course she said that she was sorry, but it was like locking the stable door after the horse has bolted.

"Hi, Coach, I wanted to apologize for ..."

"You are two minutes late! Go warm up on the trampoline," he said harshly, not like a nice grandpa as he was used to when nothing serious was going on. She understood that he would make her pay for her behavior the previous day.

She swallowed drily and went to warm up. But soon he gestured to her to stop and get down.

"So, we will start with a warning about punctuality." He bent Eve over the trampoline and, immediately, the smacking sound of a leather beater on the sporty behind of a young girl carried throughout the gym.

"What? What's this? I object! Coach, this ..." It was as if the first blow hit her ego, which was hewn by sport but also longing for success and praise. Shame washed over her, and she was shocked that she was getting a thrashing. She was used to tolerating pain—she knew how to control her body and her muscles. She could grit her teeth and work hard when she knew she was about to win. However, now, she was the one getting a spanking as if she were a small girl, and her ego was boiling mad. "How can the coach even dare this," she thought. "I am the best one, a winner. I am not a schoolgirl who forgot her homework. But the same ego kept her from breaking out and running away from another blow or from herself, the one who disappointed him.

"Remember—you agreed to take any coaching methods without bitching. The door is there, if you don't like something," he warned her calmly. But she didn't share his calmness now that she realized in what spirit practice would take place.

She didn't run away; she didn't want to—she accepted it. She considered it a punishment, not a humiliation. She trusted him. He knew what he was doing.

As he kept beating her, her eyes filled with tears even saltier than the well-known sweat, and her body was learning to withstand other landing blows. She sobbed silently and endured the rightful punishment landing at regular intervals on her stuck-out bottom, discreetly hidden within the leotard. While her whole body resisted the pain, and her adrenaline-filled intestines chose to let their contents escape. However, she ruled these physical displays with her firm hand and continued to tolerate the landing pain. Fifteen smacks transformed the color of her bottom and flooded her body with stinging pain.

Then the coach stopped and, as if nothing has happened, gave the command to practice upward jumps on a springboard by a vaulting buck. With silent sobs, Eve walked to the equipment, gripped the vaulting buck by her hands, and started with small takeoffs, going just into the air and back to the springboard. But even here, the practice was improved. The coach took a cane out of his bag, and every time when Eve was in the air, he switched her lightly. He hit her enough so she could feel it, but lightly enough that she could concentrate on jumping without hurting herself. Her bottom was raw already, and a silent ouch was a reaction to each of the ten new blows. I won't mention the number of swearwords that her angry brain made up. When he gave the command to finish, she leaned against the vaulting buck and started crying.

"Coach, I apologize. I'm sorry, and it won't happen again, I ..."

"I assume that. I wouldn't waste my time with you," he answered and pointed at the bars.

She looked down and went to the equipment. "I'm stupid, I'm stupid, I'm stupid," was running through her head. Without any problems, she swung on the rod and stayed in a first position, where she was holding in a front-support with her body stretched as a string above the bar. The coach came to her and indicated with the cane what and where her technique was wrong and how she should keep her body. Her fear of suffering another blow was great, so she really tried as hard as she could.

"Loosen and bend over the rod; it hurts more to the shortened muscles," he warned. He immediately started to thrash her and tell her what she had done wrong and how she should have been in a right position, so she would really remember it. Every blow corresponded to one mistake and worked as a brand that was imprinted on her memory of how everything should look.

After six blows, he let her get down and swing up again, and again they practiced just the opening position. And again, he struck and corrected her—this time, however, with a considerable acoustic accompaniment. Now Eve was really crying, but her athlete's pride didn't allow her to give up. She tried as much as she could, but her body discouraged her. The fear, anger, and agitation were working. She knew how to control her emotions before a competition, but this was something different. Under her leotard, twelve red stripes were hidden, and Eve bravely swung again into a requested position. Tears were rolling down her eyes, and soft sobs shook her body and made the work, which required balance, harder. Her fixed stare tried to find balance again. When she was supposed to bend over the wooden rod, she burst into tears again, but that didn't save her from another six blows landing on her painful bottom. Strength was leaving her, so she slumped on a mat and let her pain and anger at herself run its course.

She didn't care how long this practice lasted. She knew that she could manage the pain. She didn't know whether she could forgive herself, because she caused this whole situation with her ill-considered behavior. When she calmed down a bit, she found the strength to look resolutely at the coach.

He knew that she could work with physical pain, and they could stay there for a long time yet. But he didn't intend to torment or torture her at all. He just wanted to stress the importance of the situation so she didn't throw everything away on a whim.

He gave her his hand and helped her stand up. He said, "We're done for today; it's up to you what tomorrow's practice will look like." He smiled and sent his charge to a locker room. In a daze, she went to the locker room, took of her clothes, and let the soft drops of water trickle down on her. She was empty-headed and couldn't concentrate; in the end she started crying fully and angrily banged on the walls of the shower. She was mad at herself. How could she make such a wrong move three weeks before the competition? Of course, time-to-time she went out, but she had never come with alcohol still in her bloodstream before.

She took practices seriously—she took her whole sports world seriously, since she had decided on it voluntarily. This time she just couldn't handle it, and she didn't understand why. But, probably it should have been like that. She believed that everything has its reason, and so did this whole situation. She got a lesson, and she definitely needed it. She was brought to a make-or-break situation, and that was the moment when she realized what she really wanted—to stand on the winner's podium and be proud of herself. If a few welts are supposed to be a help on her way toward the target, so be it. Finally, with a smile back on her face, she got dressed and left the locker room. In front of the building, the coach was waiting for her to take her home.

The drive passed without a fuss, but when he stopped in front of her parents' house, they both took a breath to speak. They smiled at each other, and the coach started. "I do not consider today's practice usual. I just hope that it fulfilled its purpose and you found your place again. If you wanna make it in the competition, we have just three weeks to prepare. Then, if you wish to live differently, you will be free to do it. If you don't give me a cause, tomorrow's practice won't differ from normal. I know that you could bear more and that you would never beg for mercy. Athletics have taught you to grit your teeth, but that would be totally in vain if you don't change. Also, I hope that today's thrashing won't affect our otherwise good relationship. I would hate that." He finished speaking.

"Coach, I understand. I needed to get my feet back on the ground again, so it definitely fulfilled the purpose. I'm sorry that it needed to happen, and I'm sorry that I've made a misstep." She was looking at the floor of the car as she spoke.

"So everything is okay?"

"Of course," Eve replied. They shook hands with a smile, just like before the competition.

The remaining weeks were running on oiled wheels. Eve tried harder, and they polished details and adjusted exercises. They were doing everything to show her best in the competition. There was not a trace of her bad habits from the long-ago painful practice.

Was she supposed to feel humbled that a man in whom she trusted thrashed her like a small girl who was caught with a cigarette? Maybe she should, but she had no reason for that. Her ego had been hit, but she accepted the thrashing as a solution for the situation. She would feel embarrassed if he repeatedly yelled at her and scolded her about how stupid and dumb she was, and so undermined her confidence. In this way, the whole situation was finished quickly, and no one brought it up; there was no reason. It's clear that she resolved not to give him an opportunity for another thrashing.

Soon the day of the championship came. When they announced Eve's name, she was standing ready under the parallel bars. She felt her heart beating, and all other sounds went quiet. She swung on the rod, took a deep breath, and started her way to the victory. Her brain switched off as it did while the first blow with the cane had landed on her bottom. Here and now was darkness; there was only the memory of a sharp sting and a perfect execution of the first position. Every muscle worked in coordination with others, the same as when the wave of pain after a strike goes through the body in a certain way. She made a spin in a graceful motion, as if she wanted to escape another blow. Her body stretched exactly at the proper moment so she could continue with another exercise, in the same way it stretched with every blow from the cane. Everything was happening like Eve's body knew exactly what, how, and when, to move. The last exercise ended with a somersault. She did it with the same feeling of relief as when the last blow landed. A dull sound upon impact of her legs on the mat woke her up. She was standing in a straight position, and the applause of the audience rang in her ears. Her eyes met the coach's, and she knew that it couldn't have been better—it didn't matter how much the referees liked it. It was her best performance.

On the winner's podium, with a gold medal on her chest, she remembered the thrashing for the last time. She experienced the amazing feeling that she had made it, and she was able to accept her win with honor.